Alaskan Igloo Tales

Diomede
Wales
Shishmaref
C.Espenberg

George Ahgupuk

Alaskan Igloo Tales

BY EDWARD L. KEITHAHN

Curator and Librarian, Alaska Historical Museum and Library, Juneau

ILLUSTRATED BY GEORGE ADEN AHGUPUK
EDITED BY KENNETH GILBERT

Alaska Northwest Books™

Anchorage • Seattle

Library of Congress Cataloging-in-Publication Data

Keithahn, Edward L. (Edward Linnaeus), 1900-
     Alaskan igloo tales.
     Reprint. Originally published: Seattle : R. D. Seal,
c1958.
     Summary: An illustrated collection of over thirty
tales and legends from the Alaska Eskimos.
     1. Eskimos — Alaska — Legends. [1. Eskimos — Alaska
— Legends. 2. Indians of North America— Alaska
— Legends]. I. Ahgupuk, George Aden, ill. II. Gilbert,
Kenneth, b. 1889. III. Title.
E99.E7K39   1989   398.2'0899710798   89-18225
ISBN 0-88240-038-X

Original copyright 1945
United States Indian Service

Second copyright 1958
A Robert Seal Production

Seventh Printing 1990

Printed in U.S.A.

Alaska Northwest Books™
A division of GTE Discovery Publications, Inc.
22026 20th Avenue S.E.
Bothell, WA 98021

To the Native schoolchildren of Shishmaref, Alaska, who made this collection of Eskimo tales possible, I affectionately dedicate this volume as a slight remembrance of the happy years spent among them.

———*Edward L. Keithahn*

THE AUTHOR

In 1923 Ed and Toni Keithahn went to the remote Arctic village of Shishmaref to teach school, organize the reindeer herds, and to open a co-operative store for the Eskimo inhabitants of an area about 3000 square miles in extent. On many long winter nights, squatting in the cozy igloos of their new friends, they found time to listen to dozens of age-old Eskimo tales which they put down in English as close to the original Innuit as possible. This is a compilation of those delightful gems of Arctic oral literature illustrated by one of the schoolboys of that time who has since become a famous Eskimo artist.

THE ARTIST

George Aden Ahgupuk was born in 1911 in the Eskimo village of Shishmaref on Seward Peninsula, Alaska. In 1930, hospitalized at Kotzebue, he began sketching with a pencil on toilet paper. Encouraged by hospital nurses and a doctor to draw Christmas cards, he returned to his native village with $10.00 in his pocket, earned from the sale of the cards. By 1936, his drawings began to attract the attention of the art world. Since then he has found a continuous market for his drawings and has been able to make his living as an artist with a backlog of orders which would make many artists envious.

A CHAT WITH THE READER

The tales herein narrated were gathered from the Eskimo who make their homes along the Arctic coast and rivers of the Seward Peninsula. No attempt has been made to elaborate upon the original tales and the stories remain just as they were told to me except in an instance or two where our differing standards of morality make it prudent to omit some brief and unimportant details. Unfortunately the Eskimo literature is oral and the stories were not invented to be written but rather to be narrated by tribal historians who employ much action, imitation of voices and lengthy descriptions. Consequently they lose much of their value and force in the written form.

The Eskimo like other primitive people had many explanations of natural phenomena which are to whites strange and often fantastic. Because they believe those accounts rather than our "scientific" explanations, we consider them to be very superstitious. Until recent years they have accepted the leadership, not of wicked and strong chiefs, but of the "angetkoks" better known as "medicine men," "witch doctors" or "shamans." These shamans claimed supernatural powers and many Eskimo firmly believed that each "doctor" had his special "control" that would do his bidding.

However the witch-doctors on Seward Peninsula suffered ruin and disaster, according to the Eskimo, when the first white man invaded the region. According to their story, not especially designed for white men's ears, this first arrival stopped one evening with his native guide and prepared to make camp in a deserted igloo. The guide told the white man that the devil frequently stopped at this same igloo for his night's rest and suggested that they move on. The white man was obstinate, and that night as they were eating, in walked the devil. The poor Eskimo fell to the floor trembling with fright and covered himself with bedding, whereupon the devil fell upon the white man and there ensued a terrific battle. Although the devil was as hard as dried meat with all his devilish tricks he was no match for his antagonist, and realizing that he was beaten at his own game, took to his heels and left the country completely. Strange as it may seem, at that same moment all the medicine-men are said to have lost their powers. But the tales of their activities form the basis of much of the Eskimo literature and should be preserved for future generations. Most tales will be found to have a moral significance, some are merely humorous.

—**Edward L. Keithahn**
Curator and Librarian
Alaska Historical Museum and Library
Juneau, Alaska
1945

CONTENTS

THE DWARFS

In ancient times there lived among the Eskimo a race of dwarfs. E-nuk-gal-kle-nut, the Eskimo called them. They were just like the Eskimo in appearance only very much stronger and very small. They were only about as high as your knee, it is said. One dwarf alone could carry an oogrook or big, bearded seal, while two of them could launch a great skinboat and go whaling. They caught white whales and big black whales and dragged them to their igloos without the least trouble.

But there was one strange thing about these tiny people. Strong as they were, they could not move anything after it had been touched by an Eskimo.

Now it happened one day that two dwarfs had landed a large black whale. They dragged it up the hill to a shed without the least trouble. As they were about to put it in the shed an old Eskimo woman and a small boy came up and stood watching them.

"Do not touch our whale," cautioned one of the dwarfs, "for if you do we will never be able to move it to our igloos." Then the two dwarfs went away. As soon as they were gone, the woman and the little boy went to the whale and touched it with their fingers. They just had to do it, it seems. Then they went home to their igloo.

Not long afterwards, the dwarfs returned to carry away their whale. But they could not lift it. They tried again and again but it would not move. Then they knew why. Straightway they went to the old woman's igloo. They walked in looking very angry. As they came near the woman they made motions with their fists as if to strike her in the face. But they didn't touch her. They only made threatening motions and then left and never returned.

When they had disappeared a strange thing happened. The old woman's face began to swell up and her cheeks got red as if she had been beaten. Her face swelled and swelled until it became very round and her cheeks got redder and redder. And that was the way her face remained. Even to this day when you go to an Eskimo village you will still see those round faces and deep red cheeks that the people have had ever since the dwarfs punished the old woman who touched their whale.

THE FIRST BEARS

Long ago on the shores of the Arctic Ocean an Eskimo woman lived with her tribe. She already had several children but one day two children were born together. They were very strange twins, indeed. One was covered with long white fur while the other had a coat of brown fur. Since they were not like any of her other children the mother did not want them. So one day she took them far from the igloo and left them alone. When she had gone the white-furred child got up and ran down to the beach and out across the frozen sea. The brown child turned his back to the sea and scrambled across the tundra and into the mountains. And there they have lived ever since. But people do not call them men. They are known as "Nanook" or Polar bear and Brown bear.

Some Eskimo still believe them to be their cousins. This is the reason why. One time a man went hunting far out on the frozen sea. A great wind arose causing the ice to break off from the shore and move out to sea carrying the hunter with it. For many days he wandered about on the ice, starving. When he was nearly dead he saw a great white bear coming towards him. It seemed friendly and more than that, it could talk. It found food for the lost hunter and stayed with him so that he did not die.

When the wind drove the ice back to the shore the hunter asked the bear for something to prove to his friends that his story was true. The bear thereupon lifted his skin and the hunter saw that beneath it he wore clothes like an Eskimo. From his mukluk he took a string and gave it to the hunter. The Eskimo thanked the bear and it returned to the frozen sea.

When the hunter reached his village he told his story. Of course nobody would believe him. Then he took out the string that the bear had given him. Not one among them had ever seen such a string. No Eskimo could tell how it was made or how it had been tanned. And so they knew that the hunter had spoken the truth.

E-ZUM-MOL-LOOK-OON

There was once a young Eskimo named E-zum-mol-look-oon who lived with his uncle, a rich medicine-man. The time came when the uncle wished his nephew to marry but the young man could not be induced to ask any girl to marry him. Try though his uncle did, none of his scheming or magic could affect the youth, and the boy remained single.

But one day the medicine man suddenly died and went straight up into the sky, taking everything he owned with him. Ezummollookoon found himself alone in an empty igloo.

Since now he must surely starve unless he got married and could then live with his wife's parents, the young man set out to find a wife. But people had heard the news and since he was now poor no girl would consider him for a husband.

Several months later the people saw a fine kayak coming up from the sea. When it came nearer they could hear a man in it chanting and beating a drum. It was the medicine-man! He beached the kayak and going up to the igloo found his nephew sitting alone and in rags. They talked secretly for a long time then bade each other goodbye, and the uncle pushed off in his kayak and paddled out to sea.

That evening the people heard Ezummollookoon singing as he broke splinters from a piece of wood that hung from the ceiling of the igloo. "These shall be a fine wolf hood," he sang. Then he put on a tattered rabbit-skin parka. "This shall be a fine spotted deer-skin parka," his song went on.

When fully dressed the young man went out into the moonlight to look at his shadow. Yes, he was right. He looked like a rich man, now. Immediately he decided to go across the river to see the girl who had refused to be his wife. He was too poor to own a kayak so he got into a long wooden trough and taking a snow-shovel for a paddle, crossed the river to the home of the girl.

The moon was bright when he landed on the other shore and the girl, seeing him coming in the moonlight, thought that he must be rich again for he appeared to be dressed in a fine spotted deer-skin parka with a beautiful wolf hood.

Ezummollookoon approached the young woman and said, "Will you marry me now?" This time the girl consented so they went together to his kayak. First the girl got in and then the young man took his place in front of her and paddled off.

Just as they started across the river, the shovel began to talk, saying, "Ezummollookoon, Ezummollookoon's paddle is a shovel. Ezummollookoon, Ezummollookoon's kayak is a long, wooden trough."

Hearing what the shovel said, the young woman looked about her and saw that she had been deceived. For a while she said nothing, but sat still thinking deeply. When she had made up her mind she took a long wolverine ribbon from her parka and tied one end to the kayak. The other end she tied to Ezummollookoon's parka. Then she said, "I am getting seasick, Ezummollookoon. Please let me put my feet on the beach for a moment." But the youth mistrusted her and said, "No, not now. Wait until we get across the river." Again she begged him to put her ashore and again he refused. Finally she said, "Ezummollookoon, I am so sick I shall die if I cannot put my feet on the ground." The young man was frightened this time so he brought the kayak up to the shore and the girl, leaping out, ran swiftly towards her home. Ezummollookoon saw that she intended to get away from him so he sprang out to follow her but the tough wolverine ribbon held him fast. He then jerked with all his might to break it, but instead his frail wooden kayak snapped in two.

The young woman safely reached her parents' igloo and poor Ezummollookoon swam across the river as poor as ever in spite of his clever scheming and his uncle's magic.

THE ESKIMO TRADERS

Many years ago there lived two Eskimo traders. Although they were partners, one lived at Cape Prince of Wales, while the other lived far to the north at Cape Espenberg. The former traded for wolf and spotted deer-skins while the latter traded for fur.

One day the Cape Espenberg trader put a wolf skin and an Eskimo lamp in his pack and started off for Wales to see his partner. It was quite late and very dark when he finally arrived there, but to his surprise there was not a light in a single igloo of the village.

"Perhaps my partner has left me something at the council-house," said the trader and started in its direction. Arriving there he found the window plugged and all was still. Taking off his pack he pulled the plugging from the window, saying again to himself, "Perhaps my partner has left me something here."

Jumping down inside he found the room empty except for some ropes which hung from each corner. The trader thought for a moment and then taking out his knife he cut the nearest rope. Nothing resulted from that so he went to the second rope and as he cut it he heard a click. Going to the third rope he began to cut it and as it came apart there was a loud bang! and in the middle of the floor sat a bag. Upon opening the mysterious bag the trader found that it contained the head of his partner.

"I have brought you a wolf skin and an Eskimo lamp," said the trader to the head. "I will go out and get the lamp now."

"No, I will!" shouted the head in the bag.

"But I can more easily get it myself," returned the trader.

"No, I will get it," said the head and each time it spoke, fire leaped from its mouth. Finally getting tired of arguing the head said, "All right, you may go and get it," whereupon the trader went out.

As soon as he was out of the council-house, the trader, who was thoroughly frightened at the strange happenings, began to run as fast as his legs could

carry him. He had not gone far when looking back he saw a fire to which was attached a long green tail, coming after him with terrific speed. The fire was like that which had come from the head's mouth but the head had changed into a long green tail.

Just as it was about to overtake him, the trader took off his mitten and threw it at the fire which fell down and began to fight with it furiously. Presently it got away from the mitten and started again in pursuit of the trader. As it came close again he took off his remaining mitten and hit the fire with it. As before the fire fell down and rolled and fought with the mitten. Finally it pulled itself loose and ran on after the poor trader faster than ever. Soon it was up with him again, and this time would have caught him but he pulled a leg from his fur trousers and hit the fire again. Down it fell, fighting furiously, and for a long time could not follow.

Cape Espenberg was still far away and the trader ran faster and faster. Long before reaching his igloo the trader looked back and there was the fire running like the wind and steadily gaining on him. Just as the fire was about to catch him he threw his remaining trouser leg into the fire and staggered on knowing he would surely be caught now that he had nothing left that could stop the fire. But the trouser leg fought madly and the smoke rolled and the sparks flew far and wide. The trader saw his igloo loom up in the bright light of the fire and with the last of his strength dashed inside and shut the door. His wife looked at him in surprise and asked, "What is the matter? Your face looks different." Her husband could not answer. "What is the matter with you?" she repeated. "Your face looks different." The trader opened his mouth to answer. "My partner," he began and then fell dead before he could utter another word.

THE BOY WHO ATE TOO MUCH

A small boy once lived in an igloo with an old, old woman. This boy was always hungry and always begging for food. But one day the last of the food was eaten, so the old woman sent him down to the beach to search for food.

The first thing he found was a little tomcod. He picked it up and after pulling off its head, swallowed it at one gulp. Continuing his search he presently came upon a seal. As before he pulled off its head and ate the whole seal. On he went, still hungry, until he came upon a large bearded seal, or oogrook, sunning itself on the sand. Before it could scramble back into the water he had caught it, pulled off its head and eaten it. Not satisfied yet, he continued down the beach until he caught sight of a white whale stranded high and dry on the sand. In the same manner as he had done with the tomcod, the seal and the oogrook, he pulled off its head and ate the whale, skin, bones, blubber and all.

After the boy had finished the whale he felt bet-ter and presently began to sing. He rubbed his belly and sang to his stomach. For the first time in his life he had had enough to eat. But soon he became very, very thirsty so he went to a nearby pond and began to drink. He drank and drank and drank until the pond was quite dry. Then he started off for the igloo in which he lived with the old woman.

Reaching the igloo he tried to get in at the door but could not get through. He had eaten too much. "How am I to get in?" he called to the old woman. "Come in through the window," she answered. The window was much smaller than the door but he tried it anyway and found he could just get his head through. "I can't get through the window," he called to the old woman. "Come in through the ventilator!" cried the old woman in answer. This seemed ridiculous to the boy since the ventilator was very much smaller than the window but he tried it anyway. This time he got his head and shoulders through but could go no further. Again he called to the old woman for advice. "Come in thru the eye of my needle," she shouted, holding up the needle and through it the boy came tumbling onto the floor.

When the old woman saw how swelled he was from eating so much she shouted, "Look out! Keep away from the seal oil lamp!" But in spite of himself the boy stumbled towards the lamp. At the same instant the lamp sprang towards him. The old woman barely had time to rush out through the door. Boom! There was a sound like a mighty clap of thunder. When all was again still the old woman crawled up to the window and peeped in. The boy had disappeared. The lamp was gone, too. But down in the room where they had been was a deep, dark pool and in it were swimming a tomcod, a seal, an oogrook, and a big white whale.

A-PUK-EEN-A, THE GREAT HUNTER

On an island in Bering Straits there was once a large Eskimo village. The men of that village would go out in their kayaks and oomiaks in search of whales and walrus for food, but many times they would return home empty-handed. Among them, however, was a young man named Apukeena who was the greatest hunter of all. Never once did he return home without game of some sort. Even when the rest of the men could find nothing, he would bring home a seal, a walrus or a whale.

Although his parents lived in the same village this young man lived in a separate igloo of his own and with him lived his beautiful young wife. One morning the young man went hunting as usual and as game was scarce, paddled far out into the sea. There he speared a seal and putting it in the kayak behind him, started for home. He had not gone far when the seal suddenly came back to life and began to claw at his back. The young hunter saw that his only chance for life was to reach the shore, so he paddled with all his strength. The seal clawed and scratched deeper and deeper and before the kayak could reach the shore the young hunter was dead. But as he died a great storm arose and all the other hunters were driven back to the village. That evening when the hunters reported at the council-house, as was their custom, Apukeena was not there. Everyone was worried for he had always been the first to return from the hunt.

After the storm was over the young man's parents went down to the beach to search for him. The kayak had drifted ashore during the storm and when they found it there was the seal, still alive, but the body was gone. When the mother saw the blood in the bottom of the kayak she knew how her son had met his death and in her rage took her knife, skinned the seal alive and threw it back into the sea.

This act of course was a great insult to the Seal King and to punish the woman for her cruelty he caused a great flood to come. The water rose higher and

higher until the low place that the village occupied was completely covered by the sea. The waters never receded and to this day the destroyed village is beneath the sea. Only two hills stood above the water and these became Big and Little Diomede Islands.

To save themselves from the rising water some of the people got into their great skin-boats and moved to one of the hills. Among them were Apukeena's parents and his wife. They built another igloo and inside it placed a barrel in which they kept water for use in their home. But although the barrel had no leaks each morning they would find it empty. One day the mother said, "Tonight I shall hide myself and watch to see what it is that takes our water." So that night when everybody in the village was asleep she hid herself in a dark corner and watched. About midnight the old woman heard a noise. Then through the darkness she saw a shadowy, ghostlike young man drag himself up through a hole in the floor. Crawling to the barrel he pulled himself up, drank the water, and then crawled out again through the hole in the floor. Although he was as thin as death and covered with seaweed, the mother recognized her son.

Going to her husband the woman told him what she had seen. A long time they considered what was best to be done. Finally they decided they must try to trap their son. So the next day they refilled the barrel and all around it on the floor they smeared old seal oil, that had become very sticky.

That night both the mother and father watched. As before, when it was about midnight and all was still in the village, in crawled the young man, wet with salt water and covered with insects of the sea. Straight he crawled towards the barrel and was soon held fast in the seal oil. He tried to escape but was too weak to get away before his parents got to him. Then they bathed him and placed him in a new sleep-bag. Each day they fed him nourishing soup and choice bits of meat and each day his body filled out and became stronger and heavier. When he had grown until he was almost like his former self the mother went to her daughter-in-law who had not been told about her husband and said: "Please make your father-in-law a new parka for soon will come the great fete day." The young wife did as she was asked, little suspecting that the parka was to be for her own husband.

Finally the fete day arrived and all the Eskimo assembled to compete in tests of strength and skill and to dance, feast and play games. The parents went, too, but before going gave their son the new parka and told him to follow later.

When he was alone the young hunter dressed himself in the fine new clothes and went down to the beach where all the people had gathered. When they saw him coming someone said, "Look, that is he, whom the seal killed!" Another shouted, "He is the one who was drowned!" Still another shouted, "It is Apukeena, who was eaten by the sea monsters!"

When at last he stood before his wife no one could describe her joy upon recognizing her husband whom she had given up as lost.

And so again Apukeena became the greatest hunter of the tribe and his fame and strange story were known throughout the land.

THE HUNTER AND THE RAVEN

There was once a hunter who was a very poor shot. In fact, he could not even see where his arrows went when he shot them from his bow. Day after day he would hunt for caribou but never did he bring one home. The other hunters teased him about it so much that the poor hunter became ashamed of himself and very unhappy. At length life became unbearable to him so he decided to freeze himself to death. So one day when it was very cold he went far out upon the snow-covered tundra. There he took off his parka, his fur trousers, his warm mukluks and mittens and lay down in the snow to die.

Strange to say he did not freeze as he had hoped, but instead the heat of his body melted the snow away from him. As he lay there with eyes closed trying to freeze, Mr. and Mrs. Raven came by and noticing that he had no clothes on and that his eyes were closed thought that he was dead.

"Will you take his eyes out first?" asked Mrs. Raven to her husband.

"I am afraid to," returned Mr. Raven. "I don't believe he is dead."

"Oh, yes, he is," returned Mrs. Raven. "He has been dead a long time. You see the foxes have carried away his clothes."

"Yes, you are right," said Mr. Raven. "I will take out his eyes."

So, drawing out his knife, he jumped upon the man's chest to cut out the eyes. The hunter had heard their conversation and just as the raven jumped on his chest, he scrambled to his feet and sent poor Mr. Raven tumbling to the ground. The hunter caught the raven's knife as he dropped it and tried to catch the raven but it kept backing away.

"Give me my knife, Mr. Hunter," begged the Raven, but the hunter would not. "Please give me back my knife and I will pay you anything you want. When you go hunting you shall always have good luck."

"Are you speaking the truth?" asked the hunter.

"Yes," answered the raven, "You shall be a great

hunter."

"Nothing better could I ask," replied the hunter, "You may have your knife."

"Always remember this one thing," said Mr. Raven as he received his precious knife. "Whenever you kill a caribou, always take out the eyes first." Thereupon he thanked the hunter for the knife and flew away.

The man put on his fur clothes and taking his bow and arrows started to hunt again. Soon he saw a herd of caribou and easily killed two of them. Following the raven's advice he took out the eyes first, and then began to skin the animals. Presently Mr. and Mrs. Raven came flying down and after eating the eyes flew away again.

Just as the raven had promised, the man became a great hunter and for a long time always found game when he went hunting. People no longer teased him, but honored him for his great skill. But after a time he became very proud of his success and completely forgot the raven's warning. One day he killed a caribou and not troubling to remove the eyes, skinned it out and carried the meat home.

The following day he saw no caribou. The next day he was just as unlucky. The third day he saw a caribou but when he shot at it he could not see where his arrows fell. Then the hunter, remembering his previous experience, slyly decided to freeze himself. So, going out upon the tundra he took off his warm parka, his fur trousers, his mukluks and mittens and lay down in the snow. Before long the hunter was frozen stiff.

HOW A WORM DESTROYED A TRIBE

On the northern coast of Seward Peninsula there once lived a tribe of Eskimo. It was their custom each spring to leave their village and go to Cape Espenberg where they spent the summer hunting for oogrook, seal, and whales.

One spring when they departed, an old woman was forgotten and left behind in the deserted village. No food was left for her and no one to look after her. But this old woman was not ready to die even though her people thought her time had come, so each day she would go out on the beach to search for food. Sometimes she would find a piece of blubber or a fish or perhaps a piece of skin. Anyway she kept from starving.

One day as she was on her usual food hunt she happened to see a small worm in the sand and wishing a companion, for she was very lonely, picked it up and carried it home. Every day thereafter, no matter what she found to eat, she shared it equally with the worm. And as she fed it, the worm grew larger and

larger. It followed her about like a dog and soon was large enough to hunt game for her. It caught many birds and rabbits and when it was stronger would hunt in the sea and bring back seal meat for both of them.

Fall approached and the first snow was falling. It was now time for the tribe to return to the village for the winter. The worm was a huge monster by now and could kill the largest animal.

At last the oomiaks of the returning tribe could be seen in the distance. Even though they had deserted her and left her alone to die, the old woman was glad to see them returning. But the worm was not. He seemed to rage and boil within himself and the closer the boats approached, the more ferocious he became. The old woman saw it was useless to try to quiet him and it was too late to warn the people. As soon as they landed, out rushed the giant worm. The men fought fiercely with spear and bow to defend themselves but they could not pierce the thick hide of the worm. In a few moments every man, woman and child

had been killed.

The old woman had become terrified during the fight and had fled across the tundra fearing that she would be killed also if she stayed. The worm, however, did not intend to kill her. He had killed the people only because they had left the old woman to die and now he returned to the igloo to receive her thanks and to go on as they had before. But she was not in the igloo. When he found her tracks leading out across the tundra he became angry at her desertion and followed her across the snow. At nightfall he overtook her, still running, and killed her as he had the rest of the tribe. There being no one left, the village fell into ruins which you may still see. But even today no Eskimo will live at the place where the worm destroyed a tribe.

WHEN THE DEAD MAN DANCED

There was once a man named Agunaoyot. There was nothing so very interesting about this man except that he often told people that after his death he would dance. Of course this amused everybody and they laughed and poked fun at him everywhere he went. But at length Agunaoyot grew old and finally died. His body was taken to the burial place on a little mound near the beach and buried.

Several days after the funeral someone remembered what the old man had said many times and soon a crowd of men and boys gathered in the kazhgie, laughing and joking about the weird promise. Then one said, "Boys, let's go down to the graveyard and ask Agunaoyot to dance for us." Everybody thought it would be great sport so a big oomiak was filled with men and boys and they began to row towards the burial place.

As they neared the cemetery still laughing and joking, someone said, "Agunaoyot often boasted that he would dance when dead. Now we shall see if he keeps his promise!" Hardly had he ceased talking when a sharp crack was heard and looking towards the burial place they beheld Agunaoyot sitting on his grave. Fear now gripped the men and no one made a sound. Agunaoyot lifted out his left shoulderblade for a drum and a long bone from his left arm for a drumstick. Then, beating his drum, he began to dance and sing:

> "Ak-kin-a-ya-ya, Ak-kin-a-ya-ya Ah-me-le-ah-menik.
> Ka-sa-se-lu-ne Mew-mik-ilee, Mew-mik-ilee
> Eu-wa, Eu-wa-wa!"

And when the song abruptly finished, Agunaoyot suddenly lurched forward and as he did so, out of the sea came a great wave. It ran towards the boat in which the men were sitting and struck with such force that it nearly capsized. In great fear for their lives the men shouted to Agunaoyot, "Stop dancing, or we will drown!" But Agunaoyot only danced the harder, beat his drum the faster and a grin stole over his yellow

shrunken face as he continued his song. At the close of the verse he lurched forward as before and a larger wave rolled against the boat, nearly filling it with water. The men and boys tore their hair and beat their breasts, crying, "Please don't sing any more! Agunaoyot is no fool! We are the fools! If you dance again we will all drown!" The dead man only grinned at them and rattled his bones. At the end of the third verse he lurched forward and disappeared. But the ground shook and up from the sea came a mighty billow that reached nearly to the clouds. It picked up the skinboat like a feather, carried it high in the air and then swept back, drawing the boat beneath it. And that was the end of the men and boys who had laughed at a dead man.

THE ROBBER DWARFS

Many years ago every Eskimo village had a building known as the "kazhgie." This large igloo served as a council house, school, old men's home and for many other purposes. During the long winter dances were held in it nearly every night. In one village it was the custom for a dance to continue all night. Now on one of these nights while all the people were dancing and making merry, someone stole a poke of seal-oil from a man's stormshed. Since everybody had been at the dance all night they knew that the thief was an outsider, so the villagers laid plans to capture the thief. The dance went on as usual but this time guards were stationed all through the village.

In those days the Eskimo entered their igloos by means of a trapdoor in the roof. This was not altogether convenient, but it was a protection against enemies, wild animals, and above all, the cold. About midnight one young man on watch heard the sound of voices coming from the sky above him. Presently the trapdoor above him opened and in hopped two little dwarfs. The guard sprang up, shut the trapdoor and the little men were prisoners.

When the strange little dwarfs were taken to the kazhgie everybody crowded about, curious to see the dwellers of a different world. Nobody appeared angry with them and even the man who had lost his oil forgot all about it. When the dancing started, one of the men said, "How do you dance in your country? Dance for us!" So the dwarfs, who seemed quite jolly and not the least afraid, began to sing and dance:

"Hoo-way, Hoo-way, Hoo-way!
Wik-ki-kee-kee, Wik-ki-kee-kee
Ya-ka-ka! Ya-ka-kak!"

The Eskimo enjoyed the song and dance very much and everybody was laughing so hard that nobody noticed that each time the dwarfs jumped, they went higher and higher, and closer and closer to the open trap-door. All at once they gave a great leap and both dwarfs sailed out of the kazhgie.

Everybody ran outside and far up in the sky they could see the dwarfs, soaring ever higher and higher. They were returning to their own country. But even though the thieves escaped punishment they never again returned to steal oil from the Eskimo.

THE STORY OF A HEAD

Far up the Kobuk River there once lived a young man who had for a companion, a human head. Naturally, this would seem to you to be a very odd partnership, but this head was alive and could talk. Although it had no body or legs the head had the ability to go wherever it wished.

One day the two companions attended a dance in the kazhgie. When it began to get late, the young man said to his friend, the head, "It is bedtime now. Let us go home." But the head replied, "I would like to stay a little longer. You go home and I'll soon follow."

"No, you must not go alone," said the young man. "The dogs will eat you."

"Oh, no! The dogs won't eat me," returned the head. "I'll say ko-ah! ko-ah! ko-ah! and the dogs will run away. You go home and I'll soon be there."

"Very well," said the young man and started for his igloo. As soon as he had gone, the head began to think about a certain young woman who didn't want to marry anybody. When nobody was looking it left the kazhgie and rolled swiftly towards her home. When it reached the door it rolled in quietly, but not quietly enough. For the young woman heard it enter, and taking hold of its hair, whirled the head around in the air and heaved it through the open door. Out it went, but it didn't strike the ground! It didn't even make a sound but sailed through the air and landed safely at its own door. When it came in the young man awoke and asked, "How did you get home?"

"Oh, I just rolled home," answered the head, and hopped into its bed.

The next day the companions went to the kazhgie again. They stayed until late in the evening when the young man suggested that they go home as before. But the head was not ready to leave and said that it would come later.

"But the dogs will eat you," warned the young man. "Oh, no they won't!" laughed the head. "I'll just say ko-ah! ko-ah! and they'll go away."

Just as soon as his friend had left the head rolled out and down the igloo of the young woman who wouldn't marry anybody. It rolled in as quiet as a mouse but the sharp ears of the girl heard it as before. She took it by the hair, whirled it around her head, and sent it flying through the door in the roof. But it didn't strike the ground! It didn't even make a sound but sailed through the air and landed safely at its own home.

When it came in, the companion asked, "How did you get past the dogs?" "Oh, I just rolled past," answered the head, and went to bed.

The third night they went to the kazhgie and again the head refused to go home when the young man was ready. The third time it rolled out and down to the young woman's igloo. Very softly it opened the door and rolled in. The young woman heard it but didn't throw it out, feeling it would be less trouble to marry the head and end the nuisance. So the head was happily married in spite of its seeming handicaps.

Shortly after the wedding the head noticed that there was very little food in the igloo, so it said to its wife: "Tie a rope to my hair, then swing me around your head and throw me through the door. I'll show you I can hunt."

The wife tied on the rope as instructed and threw the head high in the air. It kept on going until it disappeared far out on the tundra. Before long the wife was surprised and delighted to see the head rolling back with a fine fat caribou. The young woman told the good news to her aged parents and they were all glad to learn that the head could hunt. Thereafter they not only had plenty of food but became rich.

Each day that the head went hunting the young wife would tie a longer rope in its hair in order to throw it farther. In this way it could get the bigger caribou farther distant. One day she tied on the longest rope she could find and whirled the head around and around. Then she hurled it high into the sky. Out across the tundra and over the hills it went until lost to sight. But this time it didn't land! It didn't even make a sound! And it never came back!

THE TWO ORPHANS
(A SIBERIAN ESKIMO STORY)

Across Bering Straits from Alaska on the Siberian coast lived a famous medicine-man with his wife and two children, a small girl and a smaller boy. One day the parents suddenly became very sick and in a short time the mother died. After her death the father called his children to him and said: "Do not be afraid, my little children, for when I am dead I will watch over you." Then he died and the two little children were left alone in the world.

The little children didn't know where any other people lived but the little girl took her brother by the hand and together they started out across the tundra towards a mountain they could see in the distance. That night they slept on the grass at the foot of the mountain and the next morning climbed to the top of it. And there, creeping among the clumps of tundra grass, they found a little baby. The boy was full of joy when he saw it and wanted to keep it, but while they sat there, a giant was seen coming towards them.

"Don't tell him about the baby," said the little boy.

"Let us hide it under our parkas and sit still." So the baby was hidden and both children sat still as if nothing unusual had happened.

When the giant came up, he asked, "Where is my baby?" but the little boy quickly answered, "I don't know. We haven't seen a baby up here."

"Tell me where my baby is," returned the giant, "and I will pay you well." The little girl was about to reply but her brother nudged her with his elbow and said, "But we haven't seen your baby."

Still the giant did not believe them and continued, "If you will give me my baby I will let you have my igloo on the beach. There is food in the stormshed and parkas and mukluks hanging on the wall. There is also a medicine-man's drum and a little puppy in the igloo. Around the igloo are many reindeer."

A medicine-man's drum was the one thing the little boy wanted more than anything else in the world so he decided to give up the baby. The giant seemed overjoyed to get the baby back and said: "There is

one thing that you must remember. Never beat the puppy that you will find in the igloo. Now shut your eyes and guess what I am.''

The children shut their eyes for a moment and when they opened them what did they see but an enormous black killer-whale plunging down the mountainside towards the sea, and on its back rode the baby.

Finding themselves again alone, the children started at once for the seashore in the direction of the igloo, which had been given them for returning the baby. When they finally arrived there they found everything just as the giant had promised, and the little puppy came out to meet them.

For a time the children were very happy in their new home. The girl did the housework and the sewing and the boy herded the reindeer. They treated the puppy well and even let it stay in the igloo and eat with them. The little boy liked it so much that he and the puppy were always together. But as the boy grew older he began to neglect his reindeer and would lie in bed all day beating the drum. He was trying to become a medicine-man like his father had been. But his sister now had his work as well as her own to do and consequently became very tired and cross. One day the puppy happened to get in the sister's way, and

being out of temper at the time, she began to beat it, not thinking of the giant's last warning. The puppy whined and ran outside. But the boy, instantly enraged at his sister, sprang out of bed, carrying his drum with him. Then holding the drum above his head he began to beat it and chant a strange song. Slowly he began at first, then faster and faster, and as the drum boomed with a wild, unearthly rhythm, he sank slowly through the floor. He had become a medicine-man!

Some minutes later, the boy returned through the door, smiling happily, and leading a pretty little girl by the hand. The sister did not know what to say or think but it was all soon explained. The puppy had originally been a little girl but when left alone in the igloo she had been changed into a puppy for safety. The young medicine-man's magic had broken the enchantment.

From that day on, things went well in the little home. The boy was no longer lazy but worked hard and herded his reindeer diligently. It is needless to add that when they grew into men and women the boy and the girl were married and lived happily for many years. How the little sister finally found her mate is another story.

THE BOY WHO COULDN'T REMEMBER

A small boy once lived alone with his old grandmother. In the wintertime when it was very cold, the old woman would send the boy fishing. He would make a small hole in the ice and fish through it until he had caught enough for his grandmother and himself. Then he would go home and she would cook them.

One day when he was through fishing, he lay down on the ice and looked into the hole. Away down on the bottom he saw a small bullhead. "What is your name?" called the boy.

"My name is I-ya-hu-ra," replied the fish.

"Iyahura, Iyahura, Iyahura," repeated the boy and picking up his bag of fish, started for home, running.

He had gone only half way, however, when he forgot the bullhead's name. So he ran back to the hole and asked again, "What is your name?"

"My name is Iyahura," answered the little fish.

"Iyahura, Iyahura, Iyahura," repeated the boy and ran faster than ever towards home for it was late and he was getting cold. But again, when almost to the igloo he forgot the name. Back to the hole he ran, and looking down, asked for the third time, "What is your name, little fish?" The bullhead told him as before, "Iyahura."

"Iyahura, Iyahura, Iyahura, Iyahura," repeated the boy as his breath froze on his parka hood. This time he reached the door but as he tried to repeat the name he found he had forgotten it again. Still he would not give up so he turned, took but one step, and then fell dead. His grandmother found him frozen at the door.

KING-A-LEEK, THE DUCK-SNARER

Kingaleek was a very strange old man. He lived all alone in a tiny igloo and always dressed in clothes of dogskin. He was so old that he could no longer hunt but he was able to make a fair living by setting bird snares in the small lakes nearby. Every day he would go down to a lake to take out the ducks that had got into his snares.

For many years Kingaleek caught plenty of ducks but after a time he noticed that he snared less each day. On one occasion when he visited his snares there were no ducks at all, but nearby in the grass he saw duck feathers. These proved to him that ducks had flown into his nets but had been removed, so Kingaleek came to the conclusion that somebody was robbing him of his catch.

The next day Kingaleek prepared to catch the thieves whatever they might be. So dressing in his dog-skin outfit and blackening his face with mud, he crept out through the grass to the lakes. His snares were full of ducks so he lay down hidden in the tall grass and waited in silence.

Presently Kingaleek heard a low voice saying, "You take them out." Then another low voice replied, "No, you take them out." Then the first voice returned, "Let us both take them out." Kingaleek lifted his head and looking towards his nets, saw two boys in the act of removing the ducks. Thereupon he jumped up to catch the culprits but the boys, seeing him in time, jumped up and ran across the tundra as fast as their legs could carry them while Kingaleek ran close at their heels.

When Kingaleek was about exhausted from running, he saw the boys enter a little igloo and close the door after them. So he crawled to the top of the igloo and looked through the ventilator into the room. There he saw an old man sitting with the two boys. The boys were so sick from fright and the long chase that they were vomiting but the only thing that came from their throats was the voice of the ducks saying, "Quack! Quack! Quack!"

The old man sitting on the floor was a witch-doctor, and in his anger he decided to call upon his

favorite witch to punish the man who had chased his boys. Turning to one of the boys he said, "Go get my drum." The boy jumped up, singing as he did so, "Wa-ha-ha-ha! Wa-ha-ha-ha! I'll get Mul-look-uto-keek's drum!" Then he brought the old man a very tiny drum. The man poured water on the drum and presently it began to swell up. Then he poured more water on and it became a full-size drum.

When all was ready, the witch-doctor began to sing wildly and beat the drum, boom! boom! boom! boom! boom, boom! Fire came down the mountain-side! Kingaleek saw it and started to run for home. The fire came roaring after him closer and closer. Just as it was about to catch him, Kingaleek took off a dogskin mitten and threw it into the fire. It barked and fought fiercely but the fire overcame it and ran on. Kingaleek drew off his other mitten and threw it at the fire witch. The mitten barked, growled and sprang at the fire but was soon dead. Kingaleek ran on but the fire easily overtook him again. This time he removed his dogskin parka and hurled it at the fire. It barked, growled and sprang into the fire. The two rolled and fought on the ground for a moment then the dog lay still and the fire got up hotter than ever. Kingaleek was so exhausted he was about to fall. Then he thought of his dogskin mukluks and taking them

off he dashed them at the fire. Two dogs barked, growled, then bit into the fire. It stopped a moment, grew hotter and fiercer and soon the dogs lay dead.

Kingaleek was still far from his duck pond. The only hope remaining was in his dogskin pants. He took them off and ran on as fast as his weary old legs could carry him. The fire came on, closer and closer, hotter and hotter. Just as it was about to catch him, Kingaleek hurled his dogskin pants. A double-headed dog growled, snarled and leaped onto the fire. Over and over they rolled on the ground. Kingaleek ran on, never looking behind him to see what happened to his pants. He had nothing left now that could stop, even for a second, the wild fire that soon was up and chasing him, redder and fiercer than ever. On he went—he could hear the fire roar close behind him and feel its heat and smell its smoky breath. Kinga-leek thought that surely this time he could not save himself. But just as the fire reached out a long red arm to grasp him, Kingaleek saw his duck pond and with the last of his strength, leaped into the water. The fire was running so fast that it couldn't stop and ran straight into the water and perished. Kingaleek was saved! Many years thereafter Kingaleek set his snares but never again did anyone take his ducks.

THE STORY OF AH-SIK-SO-KAK

In the vicinity of Iyak, an Eskimo village about fifteen miles west of Nome, one may see in the water a short distance from the beach a large rock bearing resemblance to a skinboat in which are seated several people. On the beach nearby are two more stones that look very much like human beings. According to Eskimo legend these rocks at one time were boat and people but due to the power of an angry witch-doctor they were transformed into stone. This is the story Eskimo grandmothers tell to their grandchildren.

Long years ago in the village of Iyak there lived a very clever witch-doctor named Ahsiksokak. With him lived his two wives, a sister and four brothers. They made their living by hunting in the summertime and by fishing through the ice in winter. It so happened that one winter day the eldest brother of Ahsiksokak and his sister were on the ice, fishing, when a storm suddenly broke upon them and carried both away on the floating ice. All winter long nobody heard from them and the people gave them up for lost.

But Ahsiksokak wanted to know the truth so all winter long he had doctored as only a witch-doctor can, and by spring had found out through his magic that his brother and sister had landed safely on a distant shore. The problem now was to get them home again.

So Ahsiksokak began at once to make the frame of a boat. When he had finished it, his wives sewed on the walrus skins and the boat was completed. Then when the little eider ducks came flying from the south, Ahsiksokak tied his brother in the boat and went out to give it a trial. Although his paddle was made from a whale's shoulder blade and the trunk of a tree, he could not keep up with the little eider ducks so he went home again. He made the boat smaller and tried it again. This time he kept up with the ducks easily so he was well pleased with his new boat.

That evening Ahsiksokak told his wives and brothers to prepare for a long voyage. They took water, clothing and much food and stored it in the boat.

Besides that, the witch-doctor told one of his wives to make a parka and mukluks just large enough for a baby beginning to walk.

When all was ready, Ahsiksokak took one wife and his three brothers and tied them in the skinboat. They they started across the ocean. The boat went with the speed of the birds and just before sunset they saw a land and the homes of many people. At dusk, Ahsiksokak changed himself into a little child just beginning to walk and his wife dressed him in the parka and mukluks she had made for the occasion and put him on her back. Then they landed and went into the first igloo at the edge of the village.

In this igloo dwelt a very kind old man and his wife. When the strangers came in, the old woman gave them food and asked them to stay and be her guests while in the village. They were very glad to stay with her, but while they were eating, a man came to the window and informed them that the chief wished the strangers to come to his igloo and play games with him.

The old woman knew that the chief meant to kill them, for sooner or later he always killed strangers who came from other villages. She was very sorry but knew she could not help them in any way.

Before the party set out for the chief's igloo one of the brothers asked if a young man and woman had drifted in on the ice the winter before. The old woman said that they had and that the chief had taken the woman for a wife and intended to kill the boy soon. Ahsiksokak, still in the form of a baby, heard her story and made his plans accordingly.

When they came to the chief's igloo they followed a messenger inside where they saw the chief lying asleep on his bed. There, also, they saw the brother and sister, neither of whom seemed to recognize them. Soon a great many people came in bearing food and then all sat down to eat. When they had finished, all of them wiped their hands and mouths on the lost brother's parka. Then the baby, Ahsiksokak, toddled over, crying, and tried to wipe off his brother's parka but while nobody was watching, whispered something into his brother's ear. The chief slept all through the evening so the brothers returned to the old woman's igloo for the night.

The following evening they were again called to the chief's big igloo. The old man and woman were very sad because they knew that the bad chief meant to kill them this time, surely. This time a great crowd was assembled but nobody sat in the center of the

room. They took seats on a bench and presently the huge chief came in carrying a heavy stone with a hole in it, just large enough to admit a man's head. This he placed against the door so that no one could enter or leave the room.

When all was in readiness, the chief announced that he would like to wrestle one of the strangers. One of the brothers stepped forward but he could not reach around the chief's waist and so was quickly thrown to the floor. Then the chief dragged him to the stone, thrust his head through the hole and broke his neck.

The second brother then faced the chief but he too could not reach around the chief's waist so was thrown and his neck broken in the stone. In the same manner, the wicked chief killed the brothers, including the one who had been lost. But when they were all dead, Ahsiksokak tore off his baby clothes and became a man again. He rushed upon the chief, locked his arms around his waist and threw him to the floor. Then he dragged him to the stone, thrust his head through the hole and broke his neck. Ahsiksokak then turned to the people and offered to wrestle anyone who was angry at him for killing their chief. But nobody came forward. Instead, many old men took out their knives and plunged them into the body of the wicked chief to show the stranger that they were glad that he was dead. Then Ahsiksokak took the heads of his dead brothers and laid them in place. He kicked the feet of each and as he did so they sprang up alive, walked over to the bench and sat down. All the people marvelled at the magic of the stranger.

Presently the people heard someone crying. The sound came from a dark corner where sat a withered old woman. As they watched she took out a small bag, untied it, and shook its contents into the air. The people were choked by a heavy, black dust that filled the room. But Ahsiksokak stood up, waved his hand and again the air became clear. The old woman in the corner was still crying. She took out another bag tied with many knots and untied them as she mumbled and wept. When the bag was open the old woman took from it the bones of a human hand. These she laid on the floor pointing one at each of the five brothers. She kicked the bone pointing at the youngest brother and immediately he tumbled off the bench, stone dead. Then she kicked the second bone and the next brother fell dead. And so they died until only one bone remained, and that pointed at Ahsiksokak. Just as she was about to kick it, Ahsiksokak jumped up, and kicking the bone towards her, the old witch fell dead. Then he touched the heads of his brothers with his toe and they again were alive. The people marvelled greatly at the strange medicine-man.

It was now very late in the night, so Ahsiksokak ordered the men to take the bodies of the wicked people out of the igloo. The body of the chief was so large that it was necessary to cut it into two parts to get it through the door. The lost sister and brother were overjoyed to see their brothers again and to be free from the wicked chief who had made them his slaves. They went with Ahsiksokak to the little igloo at the edge of the village.

On the following morning the brothers began to prepare for their journey home. Ahsiksokak was anxious to know if they would reach home in safety so he took his drum and began to beat it and chant his magic songs. He made medicine for a long while but at the end he was not satisfied with what he had found out. So he went to the people of the village and asked them if anyone could help them. He was taken to another very old woman who also made medicine and asked her many questions about the way home. The old woman went into a trance and upon coming out of it told him that there was but one way in which he could reach home safely. She told him that she would give him fire to take in his boat. With this fire he was to light a bonfire as soon as his boat touched the shore of his homeland. Ahsiksokak thanked her and departed.

Early next morning, Ahsiksokak tied his brothers, sister and wife in the boat and taking the fire, started out across the sea with the speed of the little eider ducks. Towards nightfall they reached the other shore. But the old witch-doctor who had given them the fire caused them to forget what she had told them to do. Ahsiksokak and one brother jumped ashore without the fire, and with a long rope began to tow the boat to a landing place farther up the beach. Just as they did so, the rope became rock and fell as pebbles into the sea. The boat and all the people in it turned into black stone. Even the great Ahsiksokak and his brother on the beach turned into solid rock. And there they are to this day, just as they stood many years ago in life.

ADVENTURES OF OO-GOON-GOR-O-SEOK

The Kobuk is a great river in northern Alaska. It flows westward from far in the interior to the Arctic Ocean and along its banks live many tribes of Eskimo. Most of these people live near the mouth of the river but many years ago a single family lived at its source. This family lived so far away that they had never seen anybody save the members of their own household.

The mother and father had experienced bad luck raising their family, for every son that they had, as soon as he was full-grown, would get into a kayak, go down the river and never return. Thus the parents were living alone and approaching old age when a baby boy was born to them.

The old people were very happy now for they had been lonesome. The mother fed the child on au-koo-took, which is Eskimo ice-cream and the father gave him a ptarmigan feather which he had plucked from a bird in full flight.

But the father thought of his other sons as he looked at the infant and said, "When this boy is full-grown I will kill him, otherwise he will go away in his kayak and never return to us." Then he put a crown of ermine on the baby's head. The crown as well as the ptarmigan feather had magic powers and was worn every day thereafter. When dawn came the father gave his new-born son a name. He called him Oogoongoroseok.

Happy years passed swiftly by and the boy was growing into young manhood. Then his father made him a spear and sent the boy hunting. He returned from the hunt bearing a ptarmigan that he had killed. When the father saw that his son had killed only a ptarmigan he was glad and gave thanks to the earth for he knew that his son was not yet a man.

Time passed and the father again sent his son hunting. This time he returned with a rabbit. Again the old man gave thanks to the earth for his son was still a boy. A few years went by and again the father gave his son the spear and sent him hunting. This time the boy returned bearing a caribou on his back. The old father did not give thanks to the earth this time but grew sad and thoughtful. After that day, Oogoongoroseok killed many caribou.

Along the Kobuk River are many spruce trees. When the young man went hunting he would go and return by a narrow trail cut through the forest. One day while he was away hunting, his father made a great many sharp spears. Then he dug deep holes in the trail over which he knew his son was sure to return and into each hole placed a spear pointing upwards. After covering the top of each hole with snow, the father crept behind some trees and waited for his son to return from hunting.

He had not long to wait for soon came the hunter and on his back was a great caribou. But when he came to the first hole in the trail he reached down with his spear and broke the snow away that covered the spear-pit. Then he walked on to the next hole and broke away the covering that hid it. And so he did until he had uncovered all the spear-pits, after which he went on his way as if nothing unusual had happened.

The following day, Oogoongoroseok went hunting again. When he had gone his father thought again of a plan to kill the boy. These old-style igloos had no doors in the walls but people could enter through a square hole in the roof. Just under this hole in his igloo the old man set a noose, thinking to snare his son and then shoot him with bow and arrow. That evening when the boy came in through the hole, the father gave a quick jerk but instead of snaring his son, got a bad fall for his attempt and the boy dropped to the floor unharmed. He sat down to his evening meal as though nothing had happened and the father said not a word.

The third day the father decided that he would shoot his son with an arrow so he got ready and waited inside the igloo for his return. Soon he heard a noise on the roof and as the young man dropped to the floor, let an arrow fly at him. Instead of hitting the boy, however, the arrow flew past him and stuck fast in the wall. This time the lad turned to his father and said, "You will never kill me, father." The old man was convinced at last and so abandoned his idea of killing his son.

It was not long afterward that the young hunter went to his father and said: "Father, make me a kayak." This was what the old man had long expected and feared. At first he gave an excuse that satisfied

the young man for a time but in the end he made the kayak. When it was finished he made a pair of spears to give to his son to use on his journey. The old parents were now very sad because they could see that this son also was going to leave them just as their other sons had done before him.

When everything was in readiness, Oogoongoroseok took his spears and the ermine crown that his father had given him. Then his mother gave him some aukootook to take with him, the same as she had fed him when he was a baby. Putting everything he possessed into the kayak, the adventurer bid his parents farewell and started down the river.

Our hero was well-prepared for the adventures that would soon befall him on his journey down the river. Besides possessing a large and powerful body he had the ermine crown which he had but to remove from his head to become a weasel. Or by merely tasting the aukootook which his mother had prepared for him, he was forewarned of any danger that might exist. He had not gone far when a spotted seal came up beside his kayak. Oogoongoroseok speared it and when he had placed it in the kayak behind him, continued down the river. Presently he saw a small igloo beside the river. A woman was working nearby but when she saw the kayak approaching went into the igloo. There was something suspicious about her actions so the young man tasted the aukootook and then said to himself, "There is danger here." He was no coward, however, so he paddled up, got out of the kayak and walked up to the igloo. Beside it he saw a kayak, built exactly like his own, but now old and broken. Then he climbed on top of the igloo and looked down the ventilator. The woman was in bed apparently asleep. After one glance, the young man climbed down, returned to his kayak, got the seal's head and went back to the igloo. First he walked through the narrow passageway to the door of the living room. He opened the door, pushed the seal head in toward the woman and then closing the door started away as fast as he could go. But when he turned around he found that the hall was dark and the door to the passage had disappeared! Feeling around carefully he soon found a small hole in the wall. Then taking the ermine crown off his head he became a weasel and crawled out through the hole. Once outside he became a man again and climbed upon the igloo. When he looked down through the ventilator this time he saw a spotted seal and the woman fighting each other. They continued to fight until both were dead. Then the adventurer went back to his kayak, got in, and was soon floating down the enchanted river.

About noon the young man saw another igloo on the river bank. He took out the aukootook which his mother had prepared for him and when he had tasted it said, "There is danger." As before he got out of his kayak and walked toward the igloo. A young woman who had been working near the igloo led him inside. In the room sat a withered old woman beside a seal oil lamp and above the lamp hung a big knife. He was invited to eat the evening meal with the two women and as it was getting dark decided to spend the night there. So when it was bedtime he got into his sleeping-bag and the women each got into theirs. But the young man did not go to sleep. He waited until he was sure both women were asleep and then creeping to where the young woman slept, cut off her hair and put it on his head. Then he took the crown and put it on the girl's head When he had done this he crept back into his sleeping-bag.

Not long after that the old woman got up and lit the seal oil lamp. Taking the big knife she went to the young man and whispered to herself, "This is my daughter." Then she went to the daughter and whispered, "This is the young man," and without another word cut off her daughter's head. Believing she had killed the man, the old woman put the knife in its place and crawled back into her sleeping-bag.

As soon as she was snoring, Oogoongoroseok took the crown from the dead woman's head, put it on and went quietly out to the hall. The passage was dark and the door had disappeared as before. But he took off his crown, and becoming a weasel, ran about until he found a hole large enough to crawl through. Once outside, he became a man again and started for the river. Hardly had he left when a big, black bear burst out of the igloo and took after him. The bear was furious. It tore up the earth and crashed through the willows. Oogoongoroseok got into his kayak just in time to save himself. As he paddled down the river he heard the bear calling after him in the voice of the old woman, "Oo-goon-gor-o-seok, Pee-keek-ro-seck foolish!"

Before he had gone many miles, the young man saw another igloo beside the river. He tasted the aukootook and it again warned him of danger but he could see no people about. He got out of his kayak and as he came near the igloo he saw several old broken kayaks lying on the ground. They were just like the one his father had made for him so he began to suspect the reason his brothers had not returned to their home at the head of the river. No doubt some powerful medicine-man had bewitched the whole river. The igloo he found unoccupied and there was nothing there except a harpoon. But he had hardly entered when a man came through the door. Oogoongoroseok flung the harpoon at him, but the man got away. He ran out in pursuit but saw nothing except a trail leading away from the river which he decided to follow. Before long he saw a village and when he came to the first igloo, he went inside. An old witch was alone in the room. He could take no chances now, so he killed the witch at once, skinned her face and put the skin over his own face. Then he dressed in her clothes, hid the body under a bed and sat down in her place.

While he waited there, two young men came in carrying caribou skins. Taking him for the old witch one of the men said, "Our hunter was struck by his harpoon. He is very sick." Imitating the old witch's voice, Oogoongoroseok said, "I will go to see him. Show me where he is."

The two men led him to the kazhgie where the wounded man lay on the floor. On the benches sat many people. When he had seated himself beside the wounded man, he said to the people, "Let the lights be put out." When it was dark he said, "Now sing my song." An old man in the corner began a song and the rest took it up. While all were singing, Oogoongoroseok killed the wounded man, and then taking off the witch's clothing, ran out of the kazhgie. And as he ran, wolves and wolverines came out of the kazhgie and chased him to the river. But again he escaped and paddled on down the Kobuk.

This time he had not gone far when he saw a pretty, round thing hanging in a tree. Being curious to know what it was, the young man got out of his kayak, and going up to the tree, touched the object with his paddle. Instantly the pretty thing caught him and held him so that he could not get away. Presently he heard someone coming, so he lay down on the ground pretending he was dead. A man came up and seeing Oogoongoroseok lying on the ground thought that he was dead. He thanked his trap for catching the young man and, picking him up, carried him away on his back.

As the man approached his igloo, two small boys ran out to meet their father. They were proud of him and happy because he had trapped the young traveler. The man took him inside the igloo and laid him on a bench and beside his head placed a large stone. Then he sat down to rest but soon fell fast asleep. The two boys played on the floor but after a while they too became sleepy and went to bed. Then the young traveler arose and taking the stone, hit the man on the head and ran quickly from the igloo. When he was safe outside he climbed on top the igloo and looked in at the ventilator. Two cub bears were fighting fiercely and on the floor lay a big bear, dead. Oogoongoroseok ran down to his kayak and was soon drifting down the river.

Nothing unusual happened on the rest of the journey down the river, so when it flowed out into Kotzebue Sound, the young adventurer continued on across the bay and headed for Cape Espenberg. Here he saw two tall caches and a single igloo. So he pulled his kayak up on the beach and went up to the igloo. Here he found an old man with his wife and a beautiful daughter. Nobody else lived there. The young traveler felt that this was the end of his journey and made up his mind to stay with these people. Needless to say he fell in love with the daughter and in the course of time they were married. It was a good place to live, for in the water were many seal and walrus and on the tundra roamed great herds of caribou. Oogoongoroseok hunted every day and killed many animals on land and in the sea.

One day his father-in-law pointed towards a mountain with twin peaks and said, "Don't go to that mountain when you are hunting. There are two fierce dogs there." But as there was a slight difference in their languages, Oogoongoroseok didn't understand him correctly. So it was not long before he happened to follow a herd of caribou to the double mountain and there he met with two large, fierce dogs. When they ran at him, the young man killed them with his spear. That night while the family was eating the evening meal, he said, "Today while I was hunting near the double mountain two big dogs chased me and I killed them with my spear." When he had finished the old man hung his head in sorrow and then said, "You have killed my hunters, who were the same to me as sons." Then he hung his head again and would not eat. After a while a revengeful look came upon his face and the young hunter saw that he must look for trouble.

Oogoongoroseok had lived at the Cape for a year. One day his wife was moved to the stormshed and that night a baby boy was born. The young father was happy because his wife had given him a son. The following morning the old man said, "Son-in-law, I have no skin-boat." The young man asked his wife to interpret what her father had said. She replied, "He says he has no skin-boat." Then he asked, "Where is the wood for the frame?" His wife told him where her father said he had a large log. But before he went after it, he tasted the aukootook. It warned him there would be danger.

The young man started down the beach to the place indicated. Soon he saw a big log in the sand. It had many large thick branches on it and around it were the bones of many men. Oogoongoroseok struck one of the branches with the heavy wooden mallet that he carried. As he did so the log sprang at him. He dodged the log and struck another branch. Again the log sprang up and tried to crush him but he was too quick for it. Then in anger he beat and pounded the log until it began to crack up. In a short time he had broken up enough wood for the boat frame. When he returned to the igloo and said he had broken up the log his father-in-law was very much surprised.

The next day, the young man made the boat frame and the old man said as they were eating, "Son-in-law, the boat has no skin." When his wife interpreted what he had said, Oogoongoroseok asked, "Where are the skins?" She replied that there were none so he got into his kayak and went hunting for walrus. When he had killed enough to cover the boat he tasted the aukootook before starting home. Again it told him to look out for danger.

Nothing happened until he was very close to shore. Then he saw a pretty, round thing just like the one that had trapped him up the river, hanging from one of the caches. All at once it dropped to the ground and as it did so an offshore wind came up and the sea boiled white. The young man tried to reach the shore but he could make no headway. Finally he had an idea and, blowing his breath towards the igloo, he caused the wind to go down and the sea to quiet. He then landed and skinned the walrus. When the skins were dry he put them on the frame and the boat was finished.

A few days later the old woman made some aukootook for her husband. Then the old man built a fire in the kazhgie and asked his son-in-law to go there with him. The young man, not sensing anything wrong went, but no sooner had he dropped inside than the old man shut the hole and he found himself trapped. While he was trying to get out, the wicked father-in-law appeared at a small window in the roof and poured the aukootook that his wife had made, upon the fire. Instantly flames shot up fiercely and the old man went away to let his son-in-law perish in the flames. When Oogoongoroseok saw that escape was impossible he took off his ermine crown and became a weasel. Then hiding behind the sods of the walls he waited until the fire had burned out and again resumed his own shape. When the old man returned to view the ashes of the young man he was amazed to see him sitting coolly on the bench as though nothing had happened. Neither said anything of the matter, and the two walked home together.

When summer came the young man decided to visit his old parents at the head of the Kobuk. So he packed his belongings into the oomiak, or skinboat, and taking his wife and child, rounded Cape Espenberg and headed across Kotzebue Sound towards the mouth of the Kobuk. They had not gone far, however, when a storm arose and threatened to wreck them. The young man tried to turn back but it was impossible to go in any direction. He threw pokes of seal oil overboard to quiet the waves but they only grew higher. Then he threw his property overboard to lighten the boat, but the sea ran higher than ever. Certain now that he was bewitched, Oogoongoroseok sought to break the spell. First he threw his little son overboard. The sea raged still more fiercely. Then he

threw his wife into the water. At once the wind died out, the waves ceased to roll and the sea became as smooth as glass.

Oogoongoroseok now swore vengeance on his father-in-law. On him he blamed the loss of his wife and child and now he was certain that this was the man who had caused the death of his brothers. When he got back to the igloo he rushed in and there on the floor sat his wife and child, unharmed. He was glad to see them alive but was still determined to put an end to the medicine-man before it was too late. He would watch for his chance.

Several days later the father-in-law went into the kazhgie and built a fire. This time Oogoongoroseok shut the door, trapping him as he had been trapped. Then he poured aukootook on the fire and when it blazed high and filled the entire room, he went away. When the fire was out nothing was left of the medicine-man but his charred bones.

Certain that he would never again be molested, the young man took his wife and child and again set out for the Kobuk to see his old parents. As they went up the river they found everything had changed since he came down. The little igloos were gone and in their places were the dens of animals. When they reached the head of the river he found his parents still alive and they were overjoyed to see him again. As long as they lived they never tired of hearing the stories of his adventures down the river. Thereafter Oogoongoroseok made his home at the place where he was born.

STARVING TIME AT WALES

Years ago, before they had reindeer, the Eskimo frequently had starving times and many people would die before any food could be found. It was in one of these dreadful times that the people of Wales, then known as Kingen, were starving. There were no seal or fish in the sea and the ptarmigan and caribou had disappeared from the mountains and tundra. People were already eating walrus skins, for the dogs had long since been eaten.

In a little igloo all by themselves dwelt a poor old woman and a small girl. The old woman was much too weak to search for food but the little girl would walk the beach daily in hopes that the tide had cast up a few clams or sea snails. One day when she was searching and as usual had found nothing, a kayak suddenly came up from the sea and touched the beach near her. The man in the kayak called the little girl to him and giving her a small piece of muktuk (whale skin) and blubber, said, "Do not let the people see this, but take it home and put it in a new dish with salt water. If it does not change, eat it. But if it changes do not eat it until you can see its head and tail and fins." The little girl thanked the strange man and hurried home. The old woman was very hungry and so was the little girl but neither of them so much as tasted the muktuk and blubber although this is a great Eskimo delicacy. But they put it in a new wooden dish and poured salt water over it just as the stranger had told the little girl.

In a few minutes the whale skin began to move a little. It seemed to be alive. They poured on more water and it began to grow larger. Each morning thereafter it would need more water and before long they could see a mouth, then a tail and finally it had fins. It looked exactly like a black whale but was no larger than a seal.

As the whale grew larger it became increasingly more difficult to keep it hidden from the people who occasionally came to the igloo to visit. To hide it the old woman put up a curtain across the corner of the

igloo and placed the whale behind it. The little girl's aunt visited one day and seeing the curtain asked, "Why do you have a curtain in the corner?" The old woman quickly replied, "My little girl wanted to make a playhouse so I let her do it." The aunt was satisfied with the answer so didn't look behind the curtain.

The whale grew and grew until it occupied half the igloo. One night it made so much noise that the little girl and the old woman couldn't sleep, so they felt the time had come to kill it. The next morning they cut it up and the meat and blubber filled their stormshed. Then they cooked a piece of meat and when they were just about to eat it, the aunt came in and asked where they got it. They gave her some meat and told her the story of the stranger in the kayak who had forbidden them to tell their secret to anyone.

Food grew scarcer and scarcer in the village until at last when it looked as if some of the people were going to die, the old woman let the aunt tell the people about the whale meat. When she did so, people came from every igloo bringing deerskins and whatever else they had to trade for meat. Some even died after they had eaten for they had not tasted food for many days. But the whale meat lasted until spring when the eider ducks came flying from the south and the village was saved.

THE WOLFMEN AND THE HUNTER

There was once a family consisting of a father, mother and two sons who lived alone at the mouth of a long river. Shortly after the boys had reached young manhood the parents suddenly died and left them alone. The brothers never left the old home but stayed there and made their living by hunting for seal in their kayaks.

Just across the river from their igloo, the boys one day saw a silver fox digging a hole which was to be her den. Instead of killing her, the boys daily brought her food and the fox became quite tame and unafraid of them. Early in spring a litter of fox puppies were born and when they came, the boys helped the old fox feed them by bringing birds and fish and seal meat to the den.

One day when the pups were almost grown, the two brothers were out sealing when they saw two strange kayaks approaching. The eldest brother wished to talk with the strangers but the younger one sensed danger and paddled home alone after having warned his brother to no avail. When he got to the igloo he prepared the evening meal and then sat down to wait for his brother. But the brother did not come. Night came and still no brother. The young hunter was so worried that he neither ate nor slept.

In the morning when he was about to start in search of the missing brother, a little old woman came to the igloo. "You want to know about your brother so I will tell you," she said. "Those men that you saw in the kayaks were not men. They were wolves and they killed your brother!"

When the young hunter heard this he was very sorry for his lost brother and wished to avenge his death at once. The old woman continued: "Go up the river to its source and there you will find an igloo. A little farther on is a village, and in the second igloo lives your grandmother. She can help you if you wish to find the wolf-men."

"And who are you?" asked the young man, after he had thanked her.

"I live just across the river," said the old woman, smiling. "I am very grateful to you and your brother for feeding my family." Then she left the igloo without giving the boy a chance to speak further. "It must be the silver fox," thought he, for they had fed none other.

After breakfast the young hunter got into his kayak and started paddling up the river. When he reached its source he found an igloo as the old woman had said he would. Here he left his kayak and went on until he came to the village. In the second igloo he found his grandmother who was very glad to take him in, so he made his home with her. She soon told him everything about the village. The chief man of the village had a son who was a great hunter and a very beautiful daughter who was married to two husbands. Strangely, these two men spent most of their time away from the village.

The young hunter soon became acquainted with the chief's son and the two often went hunting together. Every time they hunted, the young hunter killed game before the chief's son did. This caused the latter to admire the young man and they became fast friends.

From the day of the hunter's arrival in the village, the two husbands of the chief's daughter had been missing. In fact the people believed them to be dead.

In the meanwhile the daughter and the young hunter had fallen in love with each other and when she finally was convinced her other husbands were dead, they were married.

Winter had begun and one day while the young hunter was visiting his grandmother, she said to him, "When the winter is half over, your wife's former husbands will return from the moon. You should be on your guard for they are the wolves that killed your brother!"

When the young man heard this he was at first greatly alarmed but when he thought of his dead brother he was glad that his chance for vengeance would soon come. After that he slept with one eye open and grew more cautious as the winter went on.

One day in mid-winter the wolf-men returned but their wife warned the hunter in time for him to grasp his bow and arrows and flee to his grandmother's igloo. When he came in, the grandmother said, "You must return to the small igloo where you left your kayak. In the igloo is a spear which you must take and stick into the ground. When you have done that come back to me."

The young man did exactly as his grandmother had instructed but no sooner had he stood the spear upright in the ground than two wolves appeared and

started after him, running swiftly. He dashed away and ran with all his speed for the village. Just as the wolves were about to drag him down he reached his grand-mother's igloo. Then, turning quickly, he shot two arrows and ran through the door. "You have killed the wolf-men!" shouted the old woman. He could not believe he had been so lucky and when he opened the door to see if it were true, they were gone. But when he went to his wife's igloo, there, before the door lay the two wolves, dead.

Great happiness now filled the young man's heart for he had not only avenged the death of his brother but had destroyed his dangerous rivals as well. But when he went inside to tell his wife that he had killed her two husbands she began to weep, pitifully. "Are you sorry that I have killed your husbands who were wolves?" asked the young man. Then he showed her the bodies of the wolves and his wife forgave him. This was the first time she had known that they were wolves in the form of men and now she knew why they disappeared together for long periods of time. Needless to say, the young couple lived happily ever after.

THE TREE THAT BECAME A MAN

A cottonwood tree once grew near a river. During the long cold winter when the river was frozen and everything was still the cottonwood was very contented with life. But in summertime when the river flowed noisily by and the air was filled with birds, the cottonwood grew very discontented with its lot. It wished above all things that it could move. One day it tried so hard to walk that it actually moved! This was encouraging so it tried again and it moved easier than before. At every trial thereafter the tree moved little by little towards the edge of the river. Finally it took one step too many and fell into the water with a great splash and the swift current carried it down to the sea. When the tide came in the tree was carried high upon a sandy beach and left there.

As it lay there not knowing what to do, a bird alighted nearby and spoke to it thus, "You, Cottonwood, have two legs, two arms, and a head. Why don't you get up and walk?" Then it spread its wings and flew away.

When Cottonwood heard this he tried to move his arms. He found he could move them easily. Then he tried his legs. They moved, too. Then he got up and tried to walk. He moved slowly at first because he was stiff and afraid, but after a few trials he walked as well as any man.

While he was thus walking along the beach the bird came flying back and when it alighted said, "Cottonwood, why don't you make an igloo?" Cottonwood said, "Because I have no shovel nor wood." The bird replied: "You have lots of wood there on the beach. You can make an igloo on the hill beside the river." After saying this, the bird flew away.

So Cottonwood gathered wood along the beach and made an igloo. Then he made a shovel and covered his igloo with earth. When he had finished the bird came again saying, "Why don't you make a cache beside your igloo?" The Cottonwood man replied, "Because I have no meat or skins to put in it." Thereupon the bird answered, "Over the hill you have lots of meat

and also wolves and foxes. You had better make a cache." Then the bird flew away and Cottonwood began to make a cache. When it was finished he went up to the hill and looking down on the other side he saw a herd of caribou and many wolves and foxes. So he went back and made a bow and some arrows, and a spear and some traps. After that he hunted every day and filled his cache with dried caribou meat and wolf and fox skins.

When the cache was filled with meat and fur the bird returned and said to Cottonwood, "Make a net and put it in the river and in the winter make a hole in the ice for there are animals in the water good to eat." When the bird went away Cottonwood set to making a net and when he had finished it, put it in the river. The next morning he found that it was full of fish.

Winter came and one night the great white bears came in from the sea looking for food. They smelled the Cottonwood man's fish and started to eat them. Cottonwood saw them eating and went out and killed the bears with a club. One day he saw a dogteam approaching on the frozen river. On the sled were two young men and a young woman. When they came up to the igloo, one of the young men shouted, "Any people here?"

"Ha, yes!" answered Cottonwood. "I live here, alone." He then invited the strangers to stop with him and they readily agreed to, seeing that he had a fine new home and a cache full of meat.

Before spring came, Cottonwood and the young woman were married. She made him mukluks, mittens, trousers and parkas and was a very good wife in every way, so they were very happy.

One night when all were sleeping, Cottonwood began to snore, "Zzzz-zzzzz!" so loud that everybody woke up. "Say, what is your name?" asked one of the young men. "I have no name," returned Cottonwood sadly. "Then I will give you a name," laughed the young man. "I will name you Ka-mo-e-luk!"

Everybody laughed when they heard the name for it meant in the Eskimo language, "one who snores." But Cottonwood was glad to get any name for now nobody would ever know that he had once been only a cottonwood tree growing beside the river.

A TALE OF TWO OLD WOMEN

Two old women once lived together in a little old igloo. Food was always hard for them to get and there came a time when there was nothing left to eat. That night when they went to bed, one of the old women went right to sleep. But the other old woman stayed awake worrying about what they would do for food. All at once she heard a loud thump outside and going out found a caribou lying beside the igloo. Nobody was in sight so she dragged the deer into the stormshed. The other old woman woke up and asked, "Where did you get that caribou?" to which the first replied, "I found it beside the igloo." Then both old women went back to bed and were soon fast asleep.

For a long time the old women had meat to eat but at length the caribou was all gone and they again faced starvation. The first old woman went to bed as usual and was soon fast asleep. But while she snored the other sat awake worrying. All at once she heard a thump against the igloo and upon going out found another large caribou lying on the snow. Nobody was to be seen so she dragged it into the stormshed. As she did so, the other old woman rolled over and asked, "Where did you get that deer?" She replied, "I found it just outside our door." Then both women went to bed and were soon sound asleep.

The caribou meat lasted a long time but as they had nothing else to eat the time came when it was gone and for the third time the old women were about to starve. But the first old woman did not give it a thought. She merely crawled into her sleeping-bag and was soon snoring merrily. The other old woman couldn't sleep. She just lay awake worrying about what would happen to them now that they had no more food. Presently she heard a loud thud against the wall. She ran out expecting to find another caribou but instead, there stood a fine-looking young man.

"I have come to marry you," said the young man. Then he told her to shut her eyes. As she did so, she began to feel young and full of life and all her troubles seemed to leave her.

"Open your eyes and look down at your feet!" commanded the young man. The old woman opened her eyes, and looking down at her feet saw all the things that had made her old lying there. There was her poverty with its ragged clothes, her cares and worries and the wrinkles they had brought. All these she left in the igloo. She was now young and beautiful again.

The young man took her by the hand and together they floated up into the clouds. When they reached the top of the clouds they went thru a small hole and emerged into another land. Soon they came to the young man's igloo. When they went in the bride saw stacks of caribou skins and meat in the stormshed. The man was so rich that his wife had nothing at all to worry about.

One day the husband pointed to the hills nearby and said, "Do not go to those hills for a family lives there whom I do not wish you to see." The wife obeyed her husband very well for a time but soon she began to look towards the hills and wonder what kind of people lived over there. Finally her curiosity got the better of her and when her husband was away hunting, she stole away to the hills. There she came to an old igloo, out of which came an ugly girl in ragged and unclean clothes, who beckoned her to enter.

Inside there sat an old, wicked-looking woman who cried out in a shrill voice, "Let me see her face!" When she looked into the wife's face, everything seemed to whirl before the poor woman's eyes. Then everything turned black and she fell upon the floor in a daze. Thereupon the ugly girl took the new clothes from the unconscious woman and clothed her in rags. Then she knelt down and rubbed her ugly face against that of the young woman. Immediately her face, too, became ugly and moreover she became old and nearly blind.

When the wife finally regained her senses the ugly girl led her to the door and pushed her out. Then, groping about blindly, the poor woman stumbled across the tundra to her husband's igloo.

The young hunter had already returned and when his wife came in he knew at once where she had been. "You have disobeyed me, so you must leave," he said severely, and closed the door against her.

The wretched woman now wanted to return to the earth but she didn't know how to get down from the clouds. At last she thought of a way. First she took a large sealskin bag from the stormshed and got inside it. Then she tied it tight from the inside. When it was ready she began to roll about until at last the huge bag rolled out through the hole in the clouds and floated lightly to earth. The woman crawled out of the bag unhurt and strange to say, she was again young and beautiful. She at once forgot her sad experience in the cloudland and walked gayly along the beach. She had not gone far when she met a young man who immediately fell in love with her. She agreed to go with him to his home and in a short time they were happily married. All went well again and she was as happy for a time as she was in cloudland. However after a while she began to think about her old home and the other old woman with whom she had lived in poverty and wretchedness. Her husband warned her to stay away from the place but one day when he was away hunting she stole back to the old tumble-down igloo. No sooner had she entered than her nice, new parka changed for a ragged and soiled one; wrinkles came upon her face and her hair turned gray; her back bent and she began to worry. The other old woman woke up as she entered and then rolled over and was soon snoring peacefully. And so the two old women spent the remainder of their days; the one discontented and worrying all the while, the other happy and contented come what may.

THE WICKED MOTHER

A woman, her son and daughter, once lived all alone by the sea. The daughter was still a little girl but the son was a strong young man and an excellent hunter. He never failed to bring home a caribou whenever he went hunting.

But the mother was a very lazy person. Instead of being glad when her son brought home a deer it made her angry for it meant that she would have to cut it up, cook the meat and tan the hide. Then she would have to make thread of the sinew and sew parkas and other things from the hides. Every deer that he killed meant more work for her so at last she thought of a way to put an end to his hunting. That night when he was asleep, the wicked woman took fine ashes and poured them into his eyes. In the morning when he awoke he was blind although he could not understand how it happened.

The poor boy grieved about the loss of his sight for a long time but the mother was glad, for now she had nothing to do all day long. One day a great white bear crawled on top of their igloo and broke the window with one blow of his paw. He would have come in and eaten the people, for he was hungry, but the young man called to his mother to throw a noose around the bear's front legs. This she did, and then the boy shot at the bear with his bow. The first shot missed but at the second shot the bear fell dead. The mother skinned the bear and cooked some of the meat but refused to give her son a bit. All she would give him was seal oil and not much of that. But the little sister would always watch her chance to feed her brother when mother was not looking so he did not suffer from hunger.

Winter passed and summer followed the brief spring. One day the son asked his mother for a piece of bear meat. "It is all gone," said the wicked mother and gave him some seal oil instead. But in the storm shed there was still much bear meat. Then she took her little daughter and went out to pick berries. Salmonberries, heatherberries, cranberries and blueberries now covered the tundra. When they had filled their

baskets they carried them home. The young man asked his mother for some berries. So she put a handful of them on a wooden plate and then sprinkled them over with bugs and worms. When the boy started to eat them he felt the worms in his mouth and spit them out. However he held his temper and didn't mention it to his mother. But the little sister had seen everything and when her mother was cooking bear meat for herself, she took a piece when the woman was not looking, and hid it. After the lunch, they went out to pick more berries.

They had gone only a short distance when the little girl said, "Mother, I have forgotten my basket. May I run back to get it?" The mother replied, "Yes, but go quickly!" The little sister ran back to the igloo, and then taking the piece of meat she had hidden, gave it to her blind brother. He thanked her for her kindness and she picked up her basket and ran to catch up to her mother.

That afternoon the blind boy went out and crawled on top the igloo to enjoy the warm sunshine. And while he was sitting there he heard a loon singing and it seemed to say, "Come here, come here, come here!" The young man climbed down and walked out across the tundra guided by the loon's voice. The big diving bird was standing on the beach and when the blind boy came near it, it said, "You jump on my back." The lad got on the loon's back and they started off through the water. When they got to a deep place the loon said, "I'm going to dive four times. Tell me if you are drowning."

The blind boy held on firmly and the loon dived deep into the sea. When it came up the boy opened his eyes. He could see light! Then the loon dived again and when it came to the surface, the boy could see a short distance. The third time it dived the boy could see almost as well as before his blindness. When he came up from the fourth plunge into the sea, his sight was completely restored. The loon carried him back to the beach where the boy thanked him again and again.

When the young man returned to the igloo, he saw that there was plenty of meat left. There were baskets full of nice, clean berries. He thought for a long time and then came to the conclusion that it was his own mother who had blinded him and tried to slowly starve him. So he lay down, closed his eyes, and waited for her to return. When she finally came in he weakly asked for food and she took some berries and put them in a wooden dish. But just as she was in the act of sprinkling them with worms, he jumped up and said,

"You had better eat those berries yourself. I saw you put worms on them."

When the wicked mother hear this she tried to escape but the young man held her. After a while he said, "We must go down by the sea and hunt for seal." But it was not a seal that he wanted. He caught a white whale, tied his mother on its back, and let it go! The wicked woman was probably punished justly but thereafter whenever the boy would go hunting he would see her ride past on the back of the whale and he would feel sorry for her. After all it was his mother.

A GHOST STORY FROM WALES

Before white men came to Alaska, the Eskimo lived very differently than they do now. In those days when a boy became fourteen or fifteen years old he had to leave his home and go to live with the other boys in a large igloo called the "kazhgie." This building served as a kind of school where the boys learned the laws from the men who came each evening to talk over the day's affairs and to make or repair hunting equipment. While they worked, the boys watched and in that way learned how to make their tools and weapons as well as how to use them. There also the tribal historians would tell them the traditions of their tribe. When the evening was spent the men would retire to their homes and the boys would either dance or play games until late at night, after which they would all go to bed in the kazhgie.

This system was very successful as long as the men were in the village but sometimes when they would go away on long walrus-hunting trips, the boys who were left alone often got into mischief. And so it hap-pened at Wales long years ago, when that village still bore the native name of Kingen.

The men were all away from the village and the kazhgie boys had banded together bent on mischief under the leadership of a very bad fellow. A little girl happened to pass the kazhgie just at that time and the boys caught her and abused her in such a manner that she ran screaming to her grandmother with whom she lived alone.

When the grandmother learned what had happened she was furious and determined to punish the boys in a way that they would never forget. That evening, using the dark oil of the seal-oil lamp for a mirror, the old woman began to paint her face in the most hideous manner. When she had finished, she turned around to the girl who was still crying, saying, "There, that will scare them, won't it?"

"Oh, no, no!" cried the little girl. "That would only make them laugh." Thereupon the old woman rubbed ashes into her hair, and soot on her face. When

again finished she turned around and asked, "Will this scare them?"

"No, no, no! You can never scare them. You don't know those boys," cried the little girl.

The old grandmother tried again and again to make herself look terrifying, but at each attempt the little girl told her it would be of no use. Finally the old woman went into the corner. There she undressed, and taking a sharp knife, began to cut long gashes in every part of her body. Then she got down on her knees and elbows and crawled out of the corner towards the little girl. Blood dripping from every cut made the body unrecognizable. When the little girl looked up she gave a scream of terror. "Will that scare them?" asked the old woman?

"Yes!" said the girl. "I know that you will scare them now."

It was now almost dark. The old woman crept down towards the kazhgie. Inside the boys were singing and dancing. Among them was a younger boy who stayed there because his parents were dead. His name was Ah-me-zuk and he was the only boy who had not abused the little girl. Ahmezuk happened to go outside just as the old woman came in sight and he wondered what it could be that he saw creeping towards the kazhgie. He was a little uneasy about it, so running inside he said to the other boys, "Do not sing so loud! There is something coming!" But the boys only mocked him and changing their song sang: "Ah-me-ze-tuk suk-lum-nuvik-ta! Ah-me-ze-tuk pe-ke-ah-kun e-ke-gut ka-gunna!"

In English the song would go something like this: "Ahmezuk is telling lies! Ahmezuk is telling lies! Ahmezuk, go out and climb on a cache!"

When they had finished the song, Ahmezuk went out again and met the old woman face to face although he did not recognize her as a human being. Terrified, he ran into the room calling to the boys, "Stop singing! There is an E-ne-o-tuk outside! It walks on its elbows and knees and has eyes in its shoulders!" But the boys only shamed him for being afraid of the dark and sang about him again. The frightened boy started out to take another peep but when he opened the inner door there was the ghost already in the storm shed. Ahmezuk slammed the door shut and ran into a corner. Then he put his little fingers into his mouth, bit them, and then stuck them into a crack in the wall. Immediately the crack closed on his fingers and held him fast. The door rattled a little and the boys stopped singing and looked towards it. Slowly it opened and in crept a terrible, bloody thing. The boys could not take their eyes from it, neither could they utter a cry. They were as if stricken dumb and almost senseless from fright. The ghost crawled slowly around the room in a wide circle. Some of the boys got down and crawled around behind it. Around it went again. More boys got down on their knees and elbows and followed, helplessly. A third time the ghost circled the room and this time the rest of the boys got down and crawled behind it. All were crawling now except Ahmezuk whose fingers were still held fast in the crack. Three more times the ghost circled the room trying to get the remaining boy to follow but he held fast. Then, giving him up, the ghost slowly crawled out through the door with all the bad boys following on their elbows and knees. Across the tundra it crawled and up the mountainside until lost in the darkness.

The following morning the men returned to the village. One man, passing the kazhgie, shouted, "Boys, why aren't you having your morning dance?" Ahmezuk called to him and the man came in to see what was the matter. The poor boy was still hanging to the wall and the wall had to be cut away before they could get his fingers loose.

"Where are the boys?" asked the man.

"They were taken away by a ghost," answered Ahmezuk.

When the people of the village heard what had happened they followed the tracks of the ghost and the boys through the snow. High up on the mountainside they came upon the bodies of all the boys, each one just a short distance behind the other, and all of them frozen to death.

Those bodies were never buried for each one turned into solid stone, and there you still may see them on the mountainside just behind the village of Wales— an old and silent reminder of what might happen to that kind of boys.

WHY OLD-SQUAW DUCKS ARE EVERYWHERE

One springtime many years ago, two Old-Squaw ducks came flying into the northland. They flew like arrows and the wind whistled through their long tail-feathers as they went. They flew into the North Pacific and from there they entered the cold Bering Sea country. Then the female duck said to her mate, "Let us stop here and make our nest." "No, not yet. Let's go a little farther," answered the male and on they went.

When they had reached Bering Straits the female duck spoke again. "Let us stop here and make our home," she begged. "Just a little farther, mate," urged the male, so on they flew, whistling through the air like arrows. They entered the Arctic Ocean and flew on until they reached Cape Espenberg, just where the Arctic Circle first touches Alaska on the west.

"We must stop here," cried the female duck, "for I am almost ready to lay my eggs." This time her mate agreed, so down they swooped to earth and in the grass close to the beach began to make a little nest. When it was finished the female duck laid five pale green eggs in it.

Several weeks later the eggs all hatched out together and the mother duck led her five little ducklings down to the sea. Then she swam out into the water and the ducklings followed her. When they reached deep water the mother duck suddenly dived into the sea and never came up again. The five little ducklings cried for their mother for they were afraid, but it was no use. They never saw her again.

Finally the strongest of the five ducklings dived into the water in search of the lost mother. He swam until the water began to get very calm and shallow. At last he rose to the surface and found himself in the center of a large, still lagoon. "This is just the place for me," he thought, so he searched no further but remained thereafter in the lagoon.

The four other ducklings waited and waited for him to come back. Then the second duckling dived into the water and began to swim with all his might.

It happened that he got started in a southerly direction and as he went the water steadily became rougher and the current swifter. The sea began to narrow down and at last when the little duck came to the surface he saw a point of land running out into the sea. He was at Cape Prince of Wales on Bering Straits. Being pleased and fascinated by the rough waves and swift water he decided that this would be his home.

Three little ducklings were left at Cape Espenberg. They paddled around and around crying and waiting for the return of their mother and brothers. At last one little duck dived into the water and began to swim to the southwest. The water got rough and the current grew strong. But the brave little duck swam straight through the swift water and finally came to the surface in a quiet little bay near East Cape, Siberia. He didn't know it but he was just across the straits from his brother. But there was plenty of food for ducks here so he made up his mind to stay.

Two very worried little ducks remained at Cape Espenberg. They could not imagine what had become of the rest of the family. They cried and cried but in the end one of them dived into the water and began to swim. The farther he swam the colder the water be-

came. Then it grew dark as night. The little duck was swimming under thick, solid ice! At last he came to an open place and there he was in the very center of the Arctic Ocean! This cold, lonely place seemed to appeal to him so he made it his home and has lived there ever since.

One little duckling was left all alone at the Cape. His mother and all his brothers had deserted him so there was nothing for him to do but dive into the sea and hunt for them. So down he went and then began to swim as fast as he could. On and on he went looking here and there for his lost mother and brothers. At last, far ahead, he saw a dim light. He swam on and on until the light seemed to be directly overhead, so up he came to see what it was. It was only the sun but instead of being low in the sky as it was at the Cape, it was right above him. This little duck liked the warmth and brightness of the sun so he decided to stay right there and make his home.

So that is why, the Eskimo say, that we have Old-Squaw ducks in every bay and lagoon; in rough water and in smooth; from the ends to the center of the Arctic Ocean; and no doubt every other place under the sun.

THE RAVEN-SKIN PARKA

Once long ago, three brothers lived all by themselves. The youngest of them was very much pampered because his mother and father were dead and everybody felt sorry for him. Consequently he grew more stubborn, cross and selfish every day. In order to keep him contented the older brothers decided to make him a raven-skin parka. This pleased him very much for a raven-skin parka was very unusual in their village. But when the parka was almost completed it was found they lacked just a single raven-skin to finish it. When the little boy heard this he hurried down to the beach to look for another raven for he was impatient to wear his new parka. At the edge of the village he saw one feeding all by itself. As it was tame it was no trouble to catch and kill it. But he had hardly done so and was starting home with it when he saw an old man coming towards him, acting as if he had lost something and was searching for it.

When the old man saw the raven in the boy's hands he cried out in a beseeching voice, "Please give me my raven."

"It is not your raven!" snapped the boy. "I found it on the beach."

"Yes, that is my raven. I lost it only today," said the old man. "Please let me have it."

"No, you can't have it," returned the selfish boy. "I need it myself for there are not enough raven-skins to finish my parka."

Thereupon the old man became angry and said, "I warn you, young man, if you do not give me my raven something terrible will happen to you."

"Well, you can't have it," returned the boy as he started home.

"Very well," called out the old man, "Keep it if you wish, but if you do you will walk only a short way and then you'll sit down and say, "An-soo-gotah-tuk-tunga!"

"You can't frighten me," returned the boy and on

he went taking the raven with him. But before he had gone half the way home he began to feel very tired. His knees became weak and his limbs began to tremble so much that he was obliged to sit down to rest. Hardly had he sat down when he said in a startled voice, "An-soo-gotah-tuk-tunga!" Had he spoken in English his words would have been, "I am getting old!"

After his rest the boy got up and tried to walk. But his legs were too weak to bear his weight. He could barely crawl now, so he crawled and crawled on his knees and elbows until he reached his igloo. Not having strength to open the door he called to his brothers, "Open the door, Open the door!" The brothers heard the voice and ran to see who it was. "Pull me in, Pull me in!" cried the boy, feebly. "I am your brother."

"No, you are not our brother," said the young men. "Our brother is a little boy but you are a feeble, old man." But they took him in anyway and the boy began to tell what had occurred since he left in search of a raven. While he was telling the story he grew older and more wrinkled; his hair turned gray and then snow white and his voice sounded faint and distant. He at last convinced his brothers that he was their younger brother but during the course of the story he had grown so old that hardly had the story ended when he died of old age.

THE MAN WHO BECAME A CARIBOU

There was once a hunter who had a wife and two small sons. With them lived his mother-in-law, who unhappily found fault with everything he did. At night even, when she thought he was asleep, he often heard her berating him to his wife, telling her that he was a poor provider and not to be compared with other men in any way.

Although his wife never found fault with him, nor heeded what her mother said about him, life became so miserable for the poor hunter that he decided to leave. He gave instructions that all his nets, snares, spears, bows and arrows, harpoons and boats should be preserved for his boys when they grew up and that they should be instructed in their uses. His wife cried bitterly when he told her he was leaving but his mind was made up. He kissed her and the two little boys goodbye and started on his way.

Once alone on the tundra he began to feel very bitter toward life. Of all things on earth it was worst to be a human being, he thought. As he wandered aim- lessly about he espied a large flock of ptarmigan feeding carefree on the tundra. All about them were berries, green leaves and seeds. The ptarmigan all looked fat and contented. "Oh, if only I were a ptarmigan," said the man, "I would be happy!"

The longer he watched the ptarmigan the more his desire grew and when the flock rose like a snow- white cloud and swept away he followed them. Some- how he had a vague hope that there was a chance that they might take pity on him and cause him to become a ptarmigan. But each time that he caught up to the flock they would spread their wings and sail away. All day long he followed them hopefully. Just at sundown the flock rose over a little hill and disappeared on the other side.

When the hunter reached the spot where they had disappeared he estimated the distance that they would probably fly and just where the flock should have settled he saw a little village. So he went to the village and walked straight to the kazhgie. Inside were many men and boys and a few women. As he entered one man who seemed to be the leader or chief man of the village addressed him saying, "Why is it, stranger, that you have followed us all day?"

The hunter now saw that these were the ptarmigan in human form, so he answered, "It is because I should like to be one of you." Whereupon the leader said, "Our lives are not as pleasant as they may seem to you. Although we are always warm and have plenty of food, we are constantly in danger of our lives. We are preyed upon by birds of the air, and by beasts, as well as by men. Surely you would not like to be one of us!"

The hunter had not thought of these things which he recalled were true enough so he gave up the idea of becoming one of them. The people were very kind to him and gave him food and drink. When it came bedtime they gave him a white deerskin to lie upon and a brown one for a cover. As he was very weary from his long walk, the hunter fell to sleep instantly and knew nothing more till morning.

When the first rays of the morning sun shone over the hills the man awoke. The village and all of its inhabitants had disappeared! He looked for his brown deerskin and in its place was a brown ptarmigan feather. Then he looked for the white deerskin and under him was a white ptarmigan feather. His bed had been but two feathers, yet he had kept warm all night.

Again the hunter began to walk aimlessly about, letting his feet carry him where they would. He had not gone far when he saw a pair of rabbits frisking among the willows. He watched them for a long while as they fed and played carefree on the grass. "I believe I should be happy if I were a rabbit," thought the discontented man. "I will follow them and perhaps they will pity me and cause me to become a rabbit like themselves."

But as he approached them, they sped away like the wind. He followed them only to find that whenever he came near they would bound away. Just at sunset the two rabbits ran up a little hill and disappeared over the other side. When the hunter reached the spot where he had last seen them he looked down into the valley before him and there he saw a lone igloo. He went down to it and inside he found two old people getting ready to spend the night. They gave him his supper and when he had eaten, the old man asked, "Why have you followed us all day?"

The hunter told his troubles and ended by saying he had noticed how happy and carefree they seemed and that he wanted to be like them.

"You would not be happy if you were a rabbit," said the old man, sadly. "At times we are most miserable. Large birds of the air hunt us, to kill and eat us. Foxes and wolves lie in wait for us. Even the mink and weasel take our children. Surely you would not wish to be a rabbit!"

The hunter was convinced that the rabbits' lot was not so pleasant as he had supposed, so he troubled them no further. At bedtime he was given a sleeping-bag and in a short time was fast asleep. The early morning sun was shining when he awoke. He felt warm, yet the igloo, the old people and even his sleeping-bag had disappeared. He was alone, lying on the bare earth.

Once more the hunter started on his quest of a happy life. Presently he saw a large herd of caribou grazing contentedly on the hillside. He went closer and noticed how fat and healthy they all were. In their very numbers he saw security. There was no visible reason why he should not be contented if he were only a caribou. So he started towards the herd in hopes that they might let him join them and be a caribou. Yet as before, upon his approach the animals moved away to another spot and he had nothing left to do but follow again. All day long he followed the herd till at evening the deer went over a hill and disappeared from view.

The hunter climbed to the top of the hill and looking down before him saw a village of many igloos and in the center stood a large kazhgie. He bent his steps towards the kazhgie and upon entering found it to be full of men, one of whom they looked upon as a chief or leader.

Food was brought for the hunter and when he had eaten, the leader came to him and said, "Hunter, why have you followed us all day without either bow and arrow or a spear?"

"I did not wish to kill any of your people," answered the hunter. "I want to become a caribou and live with you."

"But why should you wish to become a caribou when you are already a man?" asked the leader.

Thereupon the hunter told his tale of woe and when he had finished, the people felt so sorry for him that they decided he could become one of their number. The next morning the hunter awoke at sunrise. The village had disappeared and all about him were caribou, kicking away the snowy cover and eating the moss that they uncovered. He looked at himself and sure enough, he was a caribou, too!

Now the hunter was happy for the first time in many years. He broke away the snow with his sharp hoofs and ate the tender white moss that lay beneath. He felt fine but at the same time he noticed he was losing weight steadily. Finally when he had become so thin that he was worried, he went to the leader and asked for advice.

"I eat all day long," said the hunter, "but I grow thinner every day."

"That is because the change of food does not agree with you," said the leader. "Whenever you eat moss, think of something you liked when you were a man." The hunter tried this plan and in a short time was large and strong again.

Everything went well with the hunter thenceforward except at times when the herd was suddenly frightened and ran wildly away. On these occasions the hunter was left far behind. Try as he might he could not keep up with the fleetfooted caribou. One day when the herd was being pursued, the leader noticed the hunter far behind and went back to him. "Why is it you cannot keep up with the herd?" asked the leader.

"It is because I lose time when I look at my feet and footing," answered the hunter.

"Never mind your feet when you are running,"

returned the leader. "A caribou looks only at the horizon when he runs."

The next time when they were chased by the wolves the hunter held up his head and looked at the horizon. He found it easy thereafter to keep up with the fastest deer.

Each night when the herd went into camp for the night, it was the habit of the leader to tell the hunter what would happen on the following day so that he would know what to do and not be afraid. One evening the leader called him to his side and said, "I will tell you about the hunters. There are two kinds. One we call the black hunter and the other we call the white hunter. The black hunter is our enemy and from him we always flee. He kills for pleasure and does not take care of his meat but leaves it to rot on the tundra. You will know him for he looks black against the horizon and when you cross his trail, his tracks prick your feet like needles. The other hunter is not really white. He is clear like water and his tracks have no scent. He kills only for food and takes good care not to waste his meat. We always try to help the white hunter."

A few days later a black object was seen on the horizon. The herd immediately took flight and as they ran, the hunter felt something prick his feet. He knew that he had crossed the black hunter's trail. When the herd was far away and out of danger the deer grazed as contentedly as before.

The following day a white hunter was seen approaching. The leader went among the deer and selecting two fat young bucks, told them to graze at the edge of the herd, which they did without question. Then the remainder of the herd wandered a short distance away and left the two bucks to the white hunter.

This occurrence worried the hunter very much but that night in the kazhgie the leader comforted him, saying: "Our boys will soon be home so do not worry." He hardly had finished when the sounds of laughter and talking came to their ears and shortly in walked two young men.

"Did the white hunter skin you properly and take good care of the meat?" asked the leader.

"Yes," returned the young men. "His knife was sharp and everything was done properly."

"It is well," smiled the leader and the young men went to their evening meal.

As the happy years went by and the hunter was now an old caribou he began to think about his former life as a man. He wondered if his mother-in-law was dead and if his wife had remarried and if his boys had grown to be strong men. As he thought of these things a desire came to him to return to his old home by the sea, so he went to the leader for advice.

The leader sympathized with the hunter and gave him instructions to follow, but warned him it would be hard to become a man after being a caribou for so many years.

So the hunter bid his caribou friends goodbye and started off towards his old home. As he got nearer the homes of men he passed by many snares and pitfalls set for caribou but he knew them and went by unharmed. But as he approached his former home he began to think about his wife and boys, forgetting all about the dangers about him. All at once he felt himself caught in a snare and could go no further. He knew that to struggle would only make matters worse so he lay down and waited quietly. Soon two young men came up and when they saw a caribou in their snare they shouted joyfully. But when they approached to kill the deer it spoke to them in the voice of a man and they became so frightened that they could not move.

"Please take me out and skin my head," asked the caribou.

For a long time the boys could not move but finally when the request had been repeated many times, one of the boys began to skin the head. When they saw there was a man inside the skin, they completed the task and the old hunter went home with the young men.

Great was his surprise and joy when his wife recognized him as her long-absent husband. She had never been remarried, expecting every day that he would return. The old mother-in-law was long since dead and the two young men who had snared him were his own sons grown to manhood.

The old hunter was at last happy to be a man but it is said that he didn't live many years as his chest was much deformed from walking like a caribou.

AN ADVENTURE OF A MEDICINE-MAN

Years ago at Cape Prince of Wales a young woman married a man who was so wicked and cruel that everybody hated him. Finally when they could bear him no longer they decided to put an end to him. For a long time they watched for an opportunity but could not catch him unawares. One day, however, some men hid in the stormshed of his igloo and when the wicked man went there for a seal-oil lamp, they caught and killed him.

After he was dead, the wicked man opened his eyes and seeing one of his own brothers-in-law, said to him, "I am sorry you were with the people who killed me and stole my lamp. Tell the people to bury me on the mountain just up to my neck so that I can see them while I am dead." Then he lay down again and closed his eyes.

According to his wish, the man was buried just up to his neck, high upon the mountainside at the rear of the village. But even though his body was buried, the wicked man's spirit went out to seek revenge. One day when the young brother-in-law was working on the mountainside the evil spirit came up behind him and shoved him over a rocky bluff, killing him instantly.

This young man had an older brother who was a medicine-man. However, this brother kept his profession a secret so nobody knew anything about his great power. The evil spirit had tried many times to end this brother's life, too, but his plots had been discovered each time.

One time when this medicine-man was out on the ice hunting for seal with a friend, the evil spirit of the dead man took the form of a polar bear and attacked him. The medicine-man fought so hard that he beat the bear off and drove him away. After the encounter he happened to see something dark lying upon the ice. Upon picking it up, he was astonished to find that it was his ear. He felt the sides of his head to see which ear was missing, and finding the right place, stuck the ear back on. But when he did so he suddenly became cross-eyed. In fact he was so cross-eyed that he was

George A. Ahgupuk.

ashamed to go home to his family. Turning to his friend with whom he had been hunting, the medicine-man said: "I am ashamed to go home like this. You go home and tell my children that I was carried away on the ice. But don't go inside the igloo. Just shout to them through the window and they will hear you."

The friend said that he would do as the medicine-man wished and bidding him farewell, started towards the land. No sooner had he gotten out of sight than the medicine-man plunged into the water through a crack in the ice. Then he swam under the ice until he came to another crack. This he passed and swam on until he came to another open place. On he went until he reached the third crack whereupon he crawled out of the water and ran swiftly home.

He had not been long in the igloo when the hunter came to the window and shouted in a loud voice, "Your father is lost! He was carried away by the ice!" Nobody answered him so the man repeated, "Your father is lost! He was carried away by the ice!" Then he walked slowly away.

When he was out of hearing the medicine-man burst out in laughter. Then he told his family the joke he had played on his friend and they praised him for his magic. After that incident he was never again troubled by the evil spirit of the dead man.

THE MAGIC BIRDSKIN

In the days of the old Eskimo nation, there was a village named Pea-nook-puk. In this village lived a man and woman who had but one son and no daughters. This son was already a young man. His parents wanted him to take a wife but he would not think of it. He was too busy hunting to let women enter his mind.

There was not another hunter in Peanookpuk who could kill as much game as this young fellow could. In summer he would hunt from his kayak for seal and oogrook and in winter he would hunt caribou on the tundra. The most mysterious thing about his hunting was the fact that he would allow nobody to go with him and no one ever came across him hunting. Yet each day he brought home lots of game.

One summer day his hunting carried him to Cape Espenberg. There on the beach he met a young woman more beautiful than any in his village. She invited him to her home so he went there with her. It must have been a case of love at first sight for they were married a few days later.

The young hunter made his home with his bride's parents as was the custom and continued hunting. He always had such good luck that his wife and her parents wondered how he hunted. They had never heard of anyone half so skillful.

About a year later a baby boy was born to the young couple and everybody in the igloo was rejoicing. Then the young mother took this opportunity to ask the secret of his mysterious hunting success. "You are the greatest hunter in the village," she said. "Please tell me your way of hunting."

"All right, I'll show you," said her husband. "Tomorrow morning ask your father to make a wooden dish. When it is finished put it on the floor and fill it with salt water."

The next morning she asked her father to make the dish and when it was completed she filled it with clean salt water from the ocean. Then she called her husband. The young hunter took from his pocket a small dried-up birdskin and placed it in the salt water.

At once it began to swell and grow larger. When it was big enough the hunter put it on. Then the skin began to shrink and with it shrank the hunter until he was no larger than a small bird. When he was the proper size he spread his wings and flew away. Presently he flew back and dropped a fish on the floor. Then he flew away again to return a few minutes later with a seal.

"That is enough!" cried his wife. "Now we know how you hunt!"

While still in the bird form the young hunter decided to fly back to Peanookpuk to visit his parents. In a short time he was there. He alighted on his father's igloo and looked down through the ventilator. He could see his parents sitting on the floor eating their evening meal. So he went into the stormshed to take off his birdskin. For some reason it wouldn't come off so he flew into the room anyway. His father, seeing the bird, tried to kill it with his knife. The bird flew around and around the room, while the father hacked at it with his knife. Finally the bird saw a hole in the wall and escaped into the stormshed.

The birdskin had been cut so many times that it came off easily this time and the son, resuming his normal size, walked back into the room. His parents were surprised to see him and glad, for they had long since given him up as lost. But when they learned that he was married and already had a baby boy they were overjoyed. Then he told them about the magic birdskin and how narrowly he had escaped just a few moments before. When they heard this, the father made him promise that he would never use the birdskin again except for hunting.

The hunter soon returned to his wife and child and as long as he lived was the greatest hunter on the coast. When he died his magic birdskin was buried with him.

A STORY OF TIYUK

There was once a young Eskimo named Ti-yuk. This fellow seemed to have a passion for hunting. He considered it a disgrace to return home without game of some kind and if he had exceptionally good luck, he would go hunting again the same day. He never rested and he never visited or danced; hunting was all that he cared to do.

It was all very well for Tiyuk to be honored as the greatest hunter of their tribe but it worked hardships on his young wife. Every seal that he brought home she had to skin and prepare for winter use. To keep up with him she had to work night and day without rest. Eventually she became so weary that she went to her husband and said, "See, Tiyuk, I can no longer wash the blood stains from my hands. We have meat in our cache to last all winter and far into the summer. Please hunt no longer but remain here and rest."

Tiyuk reluctantly consented to cease hunting but it was hard for him to do. Inaction made him restless and shortly he began to worry. At last he decided to leave his wife and home and go somewhere far away where he could hunt to his heart's content.

The following morning Tiyuk put his hunting clothes, harpoons, and knives into his kayak and started out across the ocean. Day after day he paddled on in the same direction. Each day became a little shorter than the day preceding. Finally it was so dark in the middle of the day that Tiyuk could not see the bow of his kayak.

While he was trying to decide what to do he saw a space high above him where it was daylight in spite of the darkness all around. So Tiyuk tied a long rope to his harpoon and hurled it up into the light. The harpoon stuck fast and although Tiyuk tugged at it he couldn't pull it down. This was what he wanted. Then he tied his kayak to the other end of the rope and began to climb up towards the light. Up and up he went and when he reached his harpoon he was in a new land high up on a steep cliff where it was light and sunny. He looked down to his kayak but it was so dark below that he could not see it. The cliff was so high that it was shutting out the light of the sun. So he pulled up the kayak by means of the rope and when he had it on the cliff put heavy logs on it so that the wind could not blow it away.

Being very hungry, Tiyuk sat down and ate some blubber. Then he put his small knife and other things that he would need in his sealskin bag and made ready for a long trip. His big knife was too heavy to carry so he wrapped it up and put it back in the kayak.

When all was ready Tiyuk started off across the tundra in search of people. As he walked on and on he saw many tracks of wild animals but never any of men. Once he thought he saw a village ahead of him but when he reached the place he found that it was only a grove of large willows. He went on and presently he saw some tracks of a man. They were very close together so Tiyuk knew that the man was old and feeble. So he followed the footprints until he came to many others, all leading in different directions. Tiyuk was puzzled as to which way to go. Finally he decided to walk backwards and when he got back to where the willows had been, he was surprised to find a large village in their place.

It was still daylight so Tiyuk decided not to enter until dark as the village might be inhabited by bad people who would kill him because he was a stranger. So he sat down and waited for darkness to come.

When night had fallen, Tiyuk walked into the village and looked for the largest cache. When he found it he went into the igloo nearest it, believing the owner of the cache must live there.

In the igloo, Tiyuk found a man and two women. They were very surprised to see him and the man exclaimed, "Oh, why did you come here? People never come to this village!"

"I came because my wife made me quit work," replied Tiyuk. "That is the only reason that I left home."

"All right, take off your mukluks and have some meat," said the man. Then turning to one of the women he added, "You work his mukluks and bring in some meat."

After the woman had worked the mukluks until they were soft and pliable, she went out and presently came back with several varieties of meat. Tiyuk put on his mukluks and then sat down to eat with the people.

When the meal was finished the man said, "Let us go to the kazhgie, stranger."

"All right," answered Tiyuk. "I'll go to the kazh-

gie with you."

So the two men went to the kazghie or council-room and when they entered the door, Tiyuk heard the sounds of animals in the walls. He heard wolves and wolverines; foxes, brown bears and polar bears, but he saw nothing.

The two men spent the evening visiting with each other and when it was late walked home and went to bed.

The next day the man suggested that Tiyuk should marry the young woman who had worked his mukluks. Both were willing and so they were married. As a wedding present, Tiyuk gave his wife the small knife that he had brought with him. Nothing could have pleased her more, for she had never owned a knife before. But the old man looked sad when she received the knife. Tiyuk noticed it but could not understand what was the matter.

The morning following their marriage, Tiyuk asked his wife, "Why is it that the old man seems sorry that I gave you the knife?"

"It is because he has no knife," she replied. "None of these people have knives."

"I have another knife in my kayak," said Tiyuk, "but I have forgotten where I left it."

Then Tiyuk went to the old man and told him he could have the big knife when they found the kayak. This pleased the old fellow greatly and he led Tiyuk to the kazghie.

When they entered, Tiyuk heard the animals growling as before, but saw nothing. Then the old man spoke to the voices of the wolves, saying, "Two men go get the stranger's kayak! You know where it is."

Two young men came out of the wall and went out through the door. In only a few minutes they returned saying, "We have brought the stranger's kayak. It is hanging outside on the cache."

Tiyuk was astonished when he heard that they had already returned with his kayak. "Oh!" he said, "I thought my kayak was far far from here!"

The old man asked that the knife be brought to him and when he saw it he was happy and thanked Tiyuk many times.

The following morning Tiyuk woke up feeling very unhappy. When asked what was the matter he said, "I want to go hunting. When I was home I always hunted and never rested."

"Very well," said the old man. "You shall go hunting. Put on your sealskin trousers and water mukluks. Then put your harpoon in the kayak and bring it into the kazhgie."

Tiyuk thought that the old man meant for him to take the kayak into the kazhgie that he might work on it and put it in shape for the hunt, so he brought it in.

But when he sat inside he heard a loud creaking and rending sound and the floor of the kazhgie split asunder. There, where the floor had been, was the sea, so Tiyuk launched his kayak and began hunting. When he was only a short distance from shore he killed an oogrook with his harpoon. People were watching him from the shore. Then he towed the oogrook ashore and began to cut it into small pieces. Women came and each took a piece of the meat home. When only the head was left, Tiyuk carried it home and his wife cooked it for supper.

The next day Tiyuk wanted to go hunting again. So the old man took him to the kazhgie and as before the floor split open and in its place came the sea. Tiyuk went out in his kayak and soon killed a seal. Then he killed another and another. When he had all he was able to tow ashore he paddled back to where the people were waiting. Looking back he saw that the sea had disappeared and he was in the kazhgie. Then he cut up the seals and the women came and took the meat home. When only one seal was left, Tiyuk carried it to his wife who cooked it for the evening meal.

When Tiyuk woke the following morning, he was feeling very miserable, again. His wife wondered what was the trouble and when she asked, Tiyuk said, "I am very lonesome for my old home and wife. I would like to go home but I have forgotten the way."

When he left the room, the old man asked what was the matter with the young hunter.

"He wishes to return to his first wife," replied the young woman. "But he does not know the way."

"Very well," replied the old man. "Tomorrow we will take him to the kazhgie." The old man then went to Tiyuk and told him that he could assist him in finding his home if he would follow his instructions.

"When you get into your kayak," said the old man "first paddle two strokes on the left, two strokes on the right and then one stroke backwards. Then you will be on your beach at your old home. But before you get out of the kayak be sure that you eat the four pieces of tallow that I will give you. If you do so, you will have no trouble."

The next morning Tiyuk took his kayak to the kazhgie where all the people had assembled. The floor creaked and then opened up and there was the sea! Tiyuk got into the kayak and the old man placed the plate containing four pieces of tallow in his lap.

"Now listen to what I say," said the old man. "We are not people. We are animals! We helped you because you gave us knives. Goodbye, for you will never see us again! Now, close your eyes and paddle as I told you."

Tiyuk bid everybody goodbye, then closed his eyes. First he paddled two strokes to the left, two to the right, and one backwards. Then he opened his eyes, and sure enough! He was right in front of his old home!

Tiyuk looked towards the igloo and there he saw his wife cutting up an oogrook. All at once a fit of jealousy seized him and he jumped out of the kayak and ran to his wife, shouting, "Who killed that oogrook?"

But alas! He had forgotten to eat his tallow! His wife did not recognize him and neither did she hear him speak. He shouted again and again but got no response. Finally in anger he struck his wife with the paddle and she fell to the ground, fainting.

Some people came out of the igloo and seeing that the stranger had struck the woman, drove him away, not recognizing him.

Tiyuk didn't know what to do now. At last he went to an old woman whom he had befriended many times.

When he told her his story she remembered him and was sorry. "I will try to help you because many times you have helped me," she said.

That night the old woman gave Tiyuk a strange kind of meat to eat. While he was eating it he thought the igloo and the old woman were steadily getting larger. But it was not that at all. The fact was that Tiyuk steadily was getting smaller. Things seemed bigger, and he became smaller until he fell into a deep sleep and remembered nothing more that happened to him that evening.

Tiyuk's first wife had always wanted a child but had none. That is why she readily accepted the tiny baby that the old woman brought to her the following morning. But it was a very strange baby, indeed! It wouldn't drink milk and would only eat meat from the hands of the old woman. Then it began to grow! It grew so rapidly that in three days it was a strong young man and on the fourth day it had whiskers! The second husband returned from hunting that day, and seeing the young man, recognized Tiyuk, his rival, and fled for his life, never to return.

As for the young woman, she had always hoped that Tiyuk would return, so they remarried and lived happily thereafter.

MR. RAVEN AND THE SQUIRREL HUNTER

Mr. Raven woke up very hungry one morning and started off across the tundra in search of a dead caribou so that he could eat. After walking all day without finding anything, he climbed a hill so that he could look all around the surrounding country. There was nothing dead in sight but in the distance he saw a small igloo and went toward it. When Mr. Raven approached the igloo he tiptoed up to the window and peeped in. Nobody was there but in the middle of the floor was a seal-oil lamp and over it hung a pot of squirrel-meat, cooking. He was so hungry that he went inside and helped himself to the squirrel meat. He ate and ate until his stomach was so full he couldn't eat another mouthful. Then he sat down to take his regular afternoon nap.

While he was sleeping, the owner of the igloo, who was a squirrel-hunter came home. As he came to the open door he looked in and exclaimed: ''Oh! Somebody has come from some place.'' Then he went inside and Mr. Raven awoke as he entered.

''My, but I am hungry,'' said the man to Mr. Raven. ''Come, sit down with me and have some squirrel-meat.''

''Oh, no, thanks!'' said Mr. Raven. ''I haven't eaten meat for a long time. In fact my stomach is shrinking. That is why I cannot eat meat.''

So the man sat down alone and ate his supper. When he was through eating he put his table away and began to skin squirrels. Then Mr. Raven hopped around in front to watch him work.

''Get away from here!'' shouted the man. ''You have eight feet!''

''Oh, no, I haven't,'' said Mr. Raven. ''I have only two feet like a man. Let us be friends and live here together.''

The squirrel-hunter had to admit that at times he was lonely, so he agreed to let Mr. Raven stay.

Every day the man went out and set snares to catch squirrels and in the evening he would bring home his catch and skin them. But Mr. Raven did nothing at

all. He sat around enjoying life and was always on time for his meals. At length the squirrel-hunter began to feel that this was somewhat one-sided and spoke to Mr. Raven about it.

"Now don't be angry, my friend," said Mr. Raven. "You go get me some pitch and also a good strong club."

The man got the pitch and the club and brought them to Mr. Raven, who said: "Now, my friend, I want you to invite the spotted seals to a dance."

So the squirrel-hunter went down to the sea and invited the seals to come up to a dance. When he returned a great many of them followed him to the igloo.

When Mr. Raven saw all the spotted seals he felt very glad. Then he told them to get ready for the big dance. Soon they were all dancing and having a gay time. Then Mr. Raven stopped the dance and said, "Now we will have the big surprise. Everybody close your eyes. Don't open them until I tell you ready!" When all eyes were closed Mr. Raven took pitch and poured it on their eyelids. Then he shouted, "Ready!" and the squirrel-hunter seized his club and killed them all. Not one got away because they couldn't open their eyes.

"Now, my friend," said Mr. Raven when all the seals were dead. "There are two ways to get meat and hides, so don't call me lazy any more. I may not have hands like a man, but I can work with my head."

George A. Ahgupuk.

HOW THE RICH MAN SAVED HIS PEOPLE

In the little village on Diomede Island in the center of Bering Straits there was once a very wealthy man. He had grown rich through trade with other people for he was the greatest hunter and trapper of all. In his igloo were many furs and spotted deer skins and in his caches were pokes of seal and oogrook meat.

But one winter there were no animals in the sea. The men went hunting every day but no seal, walrus or whale could be found. The people were starving. Only the rich man had food in his cache. But this man was not selfish, for in the old times all good Eskimo shared with their fellows everything they had, in times of need. So every morning the rich man's wife gave the people who came to their igloo, seal and oogrook meat that the great hunter had cached for such a time as this.

At length, however, even the good man's store was used up. There was nothing to eat now and people were dying of starvation. So the great hunter went far out on the ice in search of food. Just as he came to the open water at the end of the ice he saw a great white bear standing on the edge looking into the water. A seal came up and when it saw the bear, it couldn't move and the bear leaped into the water and killed it. When it crawled out it put the seal on the ice and began to watch the water again. Soon an oogrook came up and as soon as it faced the bear it, too, was unable to move, so the bear dived in and killed it as easily as it did the seal. Next came a walrus and then a whale but each upon seeing the bear stopped as if turned to stone and were killed by the bear.

Just then the bear turned and seeing the hunter, stood up like a man and faced him exactly as it had done the seal, the oogrook, walrus and whale. Then it blew a blast or air at the hunter. When it reached his face, the hunter felt dizzy. Then the bear blew again and the hunter fell down. The third time it blew its breath the man fainted and lay as if dead.

Presently the man came to his senses and looked around for the bear. It was nowhere in sight, so hoping that it might be in the water, he grasped his harpoon and ran to the edge of the ice. Just then the bear's head rose to the surface and the hunter hurled the harpoon. His aim was true and the bear fell dead.

The bear was so big that the hunter could not lift it from the water so he tied a sealskin rope around its neck and the other end he anchored to a piece of jagged ice. Then he hurried back to the village to tell the good news to his people.

The following morning all the men of the village followed him to the spot and helped to carry the bear and all the animals that it had killed back to their homes. The village was saved for there was enough meat to last until the birds flew in the spring.

The Eskimo people kept no exact record of time but they know that the people who were children at the time of this incident are now long since dead.

SIKSRUK, THE WITCH-DOCTOR

Once, long ago, the small son of a very rich Eskimo chief disappeared and nobody could find him. The village was full of witch-doctors, all of whom claimed great powers, but try as they might not one of them could find a trace of the boy. The parents of the boy were grief-stricken, for he was their only child.

When hope that he might yet be found was almost abandoned, an old man named Siksruk came to the father.

"I do not claim to be a real witch-doctor," said the modest Siksruk, "yet I might be able to find your boy."

"If you find him I will give you half of my wealth," said the anxious chief, grasping at the last straw.

Thereupon the old man took his drum and as he beat it he chanted a strange song. When he finished, he sat up smiling and said, "I think perhaps the animals took that boy. Maybe I can find him, though. Tell the people to gather some food for a trip and I will go tomorrow."

The chief saw that Siksruk was properly outfitted and the old man started off across the tundra alone. On and on he went towards the hills until at length he came to a very small igloo, half-buried in the ground. Noiselessly he crept to the tiny window and peeped in. Down below he saw a strange looking man and woman, and between them sat the chief's small son.

Just as he took his first look the man down below said, "Those two old women are bad women." Then without looking up he continued, "You might as well come in. We know who you are."

Siksruk wondered how the old man had seen him but got down from his perch by the window and went in the door. But much to his surprise he found the room vacant. He searched for another door and found none but in the floor he saw another tiny window. Looking down through this window he saw another room below him and in it sat two old women, no doubt the ones the man was talking about.

So Siksruk changed himself into a hair and drop-

ped lightly to the floor between the two old women. No sooner had the hair lit than the old women pointed to it and exclaimed, "Oh, we know who you are!" The witch-doctor then assumed his own form and engaged the two women in conversation.

"That man up there," said Siksruk, "just said you women are no good." At that both women flew into a rage. "If you will show me where he is now," continued the crafty Siksruk, "I will pay you with something that I have."

The old women agreed to help Siksruk and led him to a secret door that opened into the room wherein sat the man, woman and the chief's lost son. When Siksruk entered, the man looked surprised to see him and then beckoned him to sit down. "I will sing for you," said the strange man and immediately began to chant a weird song. But as he sang the magic song, things began to change. The ceiling of the igloo became open sky and in it hundreds of birds were flying. When the song was finished everything changed back and Siksruk said, "That was very good singing. Now I'll sing for you." He began to chant slowly at first, then faster and louder and wilder. "Stop singing!" shouted the man, who was becoming alarmed. "That is enough!"

"No, I'll finish my song first," said Siksruk and continued, wilder than ever. All at once he dropped his voice to a whisper and said to the woman, "Go look out of your stormshed door." Then he resumed his song.

The frightened woman went out quickly and returned at once, crying bitterly. "The sea is rolling right before our door!" wept the terrified woman. The man leapt up and ran to the door. The sea was coming in! He shut the door and turned to Siksruk pale and trembling.

"Now may I have the boy?" asked Siksruk.

"Yes!" shouted the man and woman together. "Save us from the sea and you may take him!"

So Siksruk ended his song and the sea receded. Then, taking the chief's boy, he left the igloo and started back to the village.

Great was the rejoicing when he entered with the long lost boy. The chief was overjoyed to have him back again and true to his promise gave Siksruk half his wealth which included black whalebone and many spotted deerskins.

HOW OO-VEVA-MEAK BECAME A SHAMAN

To become a medicine-man or shaman an Eskimo had first to find a "spirit" willing to do his bidding. Then he must find a way in which to call that spirit whenever he needed it. This was usually accomplished by means of a chant, accompanied by the beating of a drum. While thus chanting and drumming the medicine-man would go into a trance, or enter the spirit world, wherein he would confer with his spirits and learn things that no ordinary man could ever find out. Naturally a shaman had a great advantage over the common people and many of them became more powerful than the chiefs.

In the Eskimo village of Kingen, now known as Wales, many years ago a young man went seal-hunting on the ice and failed to return to the village. Winter passed, the ice drifted away and summer came but the young man did not come home. The people knew that he was dead. That autumn when the men were busy netting seals for the winter, a great storm arose which tore the nets loose from their anchors, and swept them away to sea. When the storm quieted the men of the village went out in boats and walked the beaches in hopes of finding their lost nets.

One of these searchers was called Oo-veva-meak. Eager to find his lost nets he wandered farther up the beach than he had ever gone before. Just as he was about to turn back he saw a man trying to pull up an oogrook. It was too large a seal for one man to handle alone so Oovevameak ran forward to give the fellow a hand. The man was so busy that he had not seen the other approaching so when Oovevameak got there it is hard to say which was the most surprised for the man was none other than the spirit of the young hunter who was lost on the ice the previous winter. The spirit rose and said, "Get an oogrook-sled and bring it to me." Oovevameak obeyed and when he brought the sled, the

two men lifted the big, bearded seal upon it. "Now," said the spirit, "you may have it. Take it home but don't tell the people that you have seen me."

"I won't tell them even if they ask me," replied the other, and so the two men parted, the latter pulling the oogrook on the sled.

Some time later Oovevameak went hunting and again his course led him to the favorite haunt of the spirit. This time the spirit came to him and said, "Let us go to my home."

"All right," said the hunter. "I would like to see how you live."

The spirit then led the way and soon they came to a deep cavern under an earth-covered glacier. This was the spirit's home. The hunter saw all about him the frozen meat of bears, caribou, seal, walrus and whale. Then there were the furs of foxes, wolves and many other animals. But what interested him most were the lost seal nets which he saw drying on racks.

When the visit was over, the hunter returned to the village. He did not tell anyone what he had seen, but stayed in his igloo day and night for a long time. People thought something was worrying him and his wife knew not what to think. But Oovevameak was not worrying. He was only working out what he thought was a very clever scheme.

At last Oo-veva-meak left the igloo and making sure that he was not being followed, walked swiftly to the cavern-home of the spirit. At the entrance stood the spirit and around its body was coiled a thick sea-serpent. "I have once been your guest," said the hunter, "now I ask that you come to my home." The spirit did not answer. "Let's go to my igloo," repeated the hunter, but still no answer came. A third time Oo-veva-meak repeated his request and that time the spirit nodded consent.

As the two men neared the village, the ground kept getting softer and softer until it was a sea of mud and the men waded up to their knees. At the edge of the village it became so deep that it looked as if the men would be engulfed in it. When it became impossible to go on, the hunter called upon the spirit for help. The spirit grinned and blew his breath towards the hunter. At once the request was granted and both men stood on firm, dry earth. But Oovevameak did not know that he must pay for each favor the spirit did him. This time the price he paid was a black spot like mud that appeared on his cheek and wouldn't come off.

So the two men entered the village. Nobody saw

the spirit for it was invisible to all but Oovevameak. The hunter went into his igloo and the spirit walked around the outer walls, whistling. People heard the whistling sound but thought it was the wind and paid no attention to it.

And so Oovevameak got the spirit that made him a shaman. His wife asked him what caused the black spot on his cheek and he told her it was black mud from the spirit of the dead man. Thereafter the spirit granted every request the shaman called upon it for, but a black spot came with the granting of each favor. Oovevameak became rich and powerful but when the black spots began to darken his soul he became cruel as well as crafty. He used his power for his own selfish purposes and was heartless in his dealings with his own people. After a time they began to hate as well as fear him. At length they could endure his tyranny no longer so the men of the village ended his life and burned his body so that they would be sure he would never come back.

TWO COUSINS

Ke-ak-e-yak lived in a village on the coast. He made his living by catching seal and oogrook and big black whales. Ma-le-yat-o-wit lived in another village about a day's journey inland, among the caribou herds. Naturally he was a caribou hunter. These two young men were first cousins and very close friends. In fact there was a strong feeling of friendship between all people of these two villages. No doubt at one time these people had belonged to the same tribe since their language, customs, dress and tools were exactly the same. Only their spears were different and these but slightly.

Maleyatowit of the hinterland was the son of a chief. Moreover, he was the best hunter in his village. Whenever he killed a caribou he would take the hide for himself and then cut the meat into pieces and give it to the people. Poor women always came to his igloo with sealskin bags for meat and Maleyatowit saw that they were given plenty. Everybody praised him.

Keakeyak was also a great hunter. He gave the poor people of his village much meat, too. But the seal-skins and oogrook oil he saved. Then when the winter snows came Keakeyak would load his sled with pokes of oil and bundles of seal and oogrook skins and drive across the tundra to his cousin's village. There he would trade for caribou skins, all spotted, which he would trade to people in his own village. Then Maleyatowit would trade the oil and skins to his townsmen who had no other means of getting these necessities from the coast. And so through this trade the two cousins became quite prosperous and looked upon as the coming chief men of their respective villages.

Keakeyak was a married man but his cousin was still single. One day the latter's parents who were now quite old, came to him and said, "Maleyatowit, we are old and have not long to live. It is our wish that you take a wife that we may see your children before we die." Now Maleyatowit wished to please his parents above all things so he decided to choose a wife. First he went to his cache and took from it many spotted caribou skins. Then he called all the unmarried women to

his igloo. Giving each of them a caribou-skin he said, "Each woman make for herself a parka. I will marry the one whose needle makes no sound."

Every one of the women was anxious to become the bride of the rich and popular trader; therefor each one sewed with her greatest skill. But it was no use. Maleyatowit heard their needles, skillful though they were.

Like all women when they sew, these women gossiped. They were talking about a certain young woman who lived at the edge of the village. One woman said that she was lazy, while another added that she had an ugly face and all of them agreed that her needle was quite noisy. Maleyatowit heard these remarks and wondered why everybody abused this absent girl but asked no questions.

Several days after the contest, Maleyatowit went hunting. This time luck was against him. He didn't see any caribou so he started home empty-handed. When he neared the village he saw a little igloo that heretofore he had never noticed and curiosity seized him. This, he thought, must be home of the girl the other women had derided.

He wanted to see if they had spoken the truth so he walked towards the igloo. Just as he was about to enter, the door opened and the most beautiful girl he had ever seen came out. When she saw him she turned and went back indoors and Maleyatowit followed. Inside sat the girl's grandmother, a very old woman who seemed friendly. Maleyatowit told them of his parents' wish and of his offer to the young women of the village. Then he asked the girl if she would sew for him. She seemed eager to take the test so the young hunter ran swiftly to his home and soon returned with some beautiful spotted caribou-skins.

The girl sat down and began to sew with the sinew. Maleyatowit listened intently but he heard no sound as she drew the sinew through the skin. He was delighted for he knew his parents would be pleased. The old grandmother gave her consent to the marriage so Maleyatowit took the beautiful girl to his home.

Shortly after the happy marriage word came from the coast that Keakeyak was lost. He had not returned from seal-hunting and his wife and children were worried. Maleyatowit felt sorry indeed for Keakeyak was his best friend. He wasted no time but went at once to the coast and inquired of his cousin's wife the way he had gone. She told him the direction and soon he found his tracks. He followed them a great distance across the ice, hoping to find his cousin still alive. But he was worried for he knew Keakeyak was too good a hunter to allow himself to be carried away on floe ice.

Presently Maleyatowit heard his cousin's voice crying, "Let me go! Let me go! My wife and children are waiting for me!" The voice came from a small tent, hidden until now by a pile of jagged ice. Maleyatowit ran up swiftly, drew open the tent, speared the two strangers that were holding Keakeyak prisoner, and released his cousin. Then they ran swiftly back to the village.

It was not long before Keakeyak had an opportunity to return his cousin's kindness. Word came to the coast that Maleyatowit had gone hunting and had not returned. Keakeyak made all haste to the hills. There was no snow on the ground but Keakeyak soon found his cousin's footprints in the grass and followed them across the tundra. On and on he went, expecting every moment to find him. But all at once the trail ended abruptly. There was not another footprint! Keakeyak circled the last track again and again but could find no more. At last, tired and bewildered, he lay down in the long grass to rest and to think. Then he saw a strange thing. Just where the trail ended the grass began to move and a small, hidden door slowly opened by itself. Keakeyak crept quietly up to it and looked in. Two big brown bears stood guarding the door but they didn't see Keakeyak. They were watching Maleyatowit who sat farther back trying to think of a way to escape.

Then the little door slowly began to close. Realizing that his chance to rescue his cousin had come, Keakeyak leaped in and speared the two bears. Both men then ran for the door which was steadily closing. Keakeyak squeezed through and Maleyatowit followed closely. Then the door snapped shut. It caught Maleyatowit's parka but he tore himself free and escaped unharmed. Thus Keakeyak returned his cousin's kindness.

These two cousins continued to prosper thereafter and when they had gray hair became chiefs in their respective villages. The villages continued to live in peace with each other and many years later when the caribou were gone, the two tribes re-united in the village on the coast.

Many men still follow Keakeyak's occupation of seal-hunting. But others, probably the descendants of Maleyatowit and his tribe, are returning to the hinterland not to hunt caribou but to herd its cousin, the reindeer.

A STORY FROM THE KOYUKUK

Far in the Arctic interior of Alaska flows the great Koyukuk river southward to meet the mighty Yukon. Along its spruce-lined banks dwell a race of people closely akin both to Eskimo and Indian. This is a story from those people of long ago; of Nasee-kayoosie, son of Ki-ou-tay-luk.

Of all the men in the village, Kioutayluk was the richest. To him belonged the largest igloo and the tallest cache. His were the strongest dogs, the finest sleds, the best-trimmed parkas. He was the one who had meat to give to the poor when game was scarce; to him many people owed their lives. So when Mig-i-nosie, his pretty wife, bore him a son, there was no end of rejoicing. People came from miles around to see the first-born of Kioutayluk. Women begged permission to take care of him; others made mukluks for his tiny feet and little parkas of rabbit fur to keep him warm. They called him Naseekayoosie, son of the great Kioutayluk.

Several years passed by. The rich man's son was old enough to talk. People showed more love for him than ever. Women made him pretty fur clothes and men carved him playthings of wood. A little sister was born one day and while the village rejoiced again, Naseekayoosie was still the favorite. He, they told him, would grow up and be a great and powerful man like his father and they would some day hear his wise words in the council-house.

Not many years after the birth of his sister, a very sad thing happened. Some strange sickness came to the village and many people died. Not even were the strongest spared, for among the victims were the great Kioutayluk and Miginosie, his wife. The little boy and his still smaller sister were left alone in the world.

Several days later some strangers came to the village and finding the motherless little girl, took her with them and adopted her into their own family. But strange to say, nobody wanted the boy. Men who had once whittled him toys of wood came and took away his father's belongings. Women who formerly had loved him now scolded him and thrust him out when he came to their igloos. Even his former playmates jeered and taunted him now. Nobody was so poor and lonely as Naseekayoosie who was once loved and admired by all.

At last the poor boy decided to leave the village where everybody treated him so cruelly. Out into the forest he went, and far from where people had ever been, made his way. The village folk believed him to be dead and soon forgot that he had ever lived.

But Naseekayoosie didn't die. Living was hard for him for he was only a boy and had never been taught to hunt. Sometimes he had to eat roots and the bark of trees to keep from starving. Sores came on his skin from eating bad food and he suffered from lack of warm clothing. But as years went by, in spite of his hardships, he grew into a strong young man. He knew very little about the ways of men but he had developed many of the instincts of a wild animal. His eyes were keen like the eyes of the great lynx and like it he could see in the dark. But if his eyes were keen, his ears and mind were keener. He could not only hear sounds that only wild animals can hear but he could even read one's mind and knew of things impending.

As Naseekayoosie became older he began to feel the urge to be among people like himself. Finally, un-able to resist any longer, he started back the way he had come perhaps ten years before. When he reached the village things were very different than they had been at the time he left. Most of the people were poor and half-starved and many of the older inhabitants had long since died. He told nobody who he was and no one showed any great interest in him. To the villagers he was nothing but a poor wanderer of their own race and being poor there was nothing to be gained from him. Nobody dreamed that he was the son of the great Kioutayluk, and if they had it would have made very little difference under the circumstances.

Since nobody was friendly enough to take him in, Naseekayoosie went to the kazhgie and lived with the other homeless men. When the women brought them food they shared it with him so he was seldom hungry. Some of the men gave him clothes and at night when the married men went home, he slept in the kazhgie with the boys and old men.

But Naseekayoosie was not wasting time. Every night when the men came to the kazhgie to work and tell their experiences, he would watch and listen attentively. The result was that soon he knew how to make spears, arrows, snares, boats and sleds as well as the best of the workers. Having learned the habits of animals during his long stay in the forest, it was not long before he was numbered among the best hunters in the village.

Several years passed by. Naseekayoosie was still living in the kazhgie. But he was no longer poor. Through his good hunting and other habits of industry he had already laid up a considerable store of wealth. His parkas were now made of the best spotted deerskins and were trimmed with the finest cuts of wolverine and wolf fur. Moreover he owned the finest string of dogs in the village. But people were whispering. The more Naseekayoosie prospered, the more jealous they became. At night when he sat in the kazhgie he could hear people talking about him in their igloos. Some predicted that he was going to be rich like Kioutayluk had been and others suggested that this might be the son of Kioutayluk or at least his spirit, returned to punish them for their treatment of his children.

For the most part, the people secretly hated Naseekayoosie. The custom in those days was to divide up with your neighbors all game of consequence or any especially good catch of anything. This custom tended to keep all people on a social and economic level, but it did not tend to encourage industry. Naseekayoosie gave meat to the hungry but he did not believe in dividing his fur with those who were lazy, and so his stock of fur increased as did his enemies. People spoke kind words to him now and smiled when they met him but Naseekayoosie knew what was in their hearts and it grieved him. He tried to remember only the kindnesses that had been done him and to forget the unkindnesses that had driven him from the village into the forest years before.

The time came when Naseekayoosie began to think of a home of his own and a wife and children. Heretofore he had lived in the kazhgie. Now he wanted to build an igloo and erect a cache so that travelers would know where they might enjoy the most hospitality. But no sooner had he entered into courtship with one of the village girls than everyone was talking. He had not been seen in the kazhgie for two nights and scandal was abroad. One old man became alarmed at the way people were passing uncomplimentary remarks and cautioned them, saying, "He, of whom you speak, is like a wild animal. He hears though he is not among us. Do not even think evil of him, I warn you, lest he hear your unspoken thoughts."

Several days later Naseekayoosie married the young woman of his choice. He built her an igloo and gave her the best of everything that was available for

barter. He loved her more than anything else in the world and for the first time since his return to the village he was happy.

After the marriage, according to custom, Naseekayoosie spent his evenings in the kazghie with the other hunters. Every evening his wife came with the food he liked best and waited while he ate. People marvelled at her devotion. But there were two young men in the village who were jealous of him and it angered them to see his wife show such devotion to him. So one evening before she came with the customary bowl of food, these two men hid in the dark, tunnel-like entrance to the kazghie. When she started to crawl thru, one man caught her sleeve, saying, "Wait a moment; we have something to tell you. When your husband comes home at night, no doubt he tells you he loves you. Do not believe him! When the kazghie is full of men, he tells them everything you do. He is making you the laughing-stock of the whole village."

When the young wife heard these words she became so angry that she ran home in a fury, carrying the bowl of food with her. The thought had never entered her head that the young men had lied to her.

Poor Naseekayoosie heard the two young men lie to his wife and it grieved him when she did not bring the food that evening for he knew that his wife could have had no faith in him else she would not have believed the plotters.

As soon as the young wife got home she told her parents what the young men had said. At once the mother was furious. But the father said nothing. Presently, after thinking it over carefully, he said, "There must be some mistake. Naseekayoosie seems not to be that kind of a man." From the kazghie, Naseekayoosie heard the conversation in the igloo and his heart was heavy.

At the evening meal in the igloo, the mother served frozen blueberries in seal-oil for dessert. This was Naseekayoosie's favorite dish, so the old father said, "Daughter, go over to the kazghie and give your husband some of these berries. He will be waiting for you." But it was useless to urge the young woman. Her anger, instead of cooling, mounted higher at each mention of her husband's name.

Bedtime came and the poor husband started home. He dreaded what he knew was before him. As he entered the igloo, his mother-in-law, who had hidden herself in the stormshed, dashed the contents of a wooden garbage pail over him. He backed out and called to some passing men to get him some clean clothes. After he had taken a bath and redressed, he went back to the kazhgie and spent the night. He was convinced that he was no longer welcome in his home.

The next morning, Naseekayoosie awoke a different man. Never before had he spoken in the kazhgie; always had he humbled himself before the villagers. This day he sent an order for all people to come and hear his message. People saw the change in him and came from all parts of the village to hear what he had to say.

When the kazhgie was filled with wondering people, Naseekayoosie rose before them, and speaking like his father Kioutayluk had spoken many times before him, said, "One year from today we shall move to a new hunting ground. Let every woman who can sew make warm clothing for her family. I will give skins to those who have none."

The people had long needed a leader. Ever since the death of Kioutayluk they had gone blindly on, foolishly wasting their game until now only a few caribou and ptarmigan remained and the people were continually in poverty. From that moment, Naseekayoosie was chief. The women began to sew warm parkas and mukluks and the men began to build new sleds, make harnesses and other traveling equipment. A good food supply was laid in and all preparations made in accordance to their new leader's wishes.

In exactly one year, the whole village packed their scanty belongings on sleds, hooked up their dogs and started off, they knew not where, but they trusted Naseekayoosie's judgment.

One family alone had not heeded the leader's warning. Naseekayoosie's wife and her parents had not gone to the kazhgie to hear his speech and when they did hear of his orders, both women scoffed at the idea and refused to sew warm clothes for the journey. But when they saw everybody leaving, they were frightened lest they be left alone in an empty village. Hastily they packed their sled and followed.

A great distance from the village, Naseekayoosie loosened the thongs that bound his sled-load and drew out a strange-looking sealskin bag. When he opened the bag, cold, biting winds came forth and the travelers hurriedly put on their warmest clothing. But the family that had not listened to the leader had not provided themselves with warm clothes. Shuddering with cold, they continued on, hoping that someone would have pity on them. Soon, however, the leader drew out the mysterious bag again. Colder, fiercer winds came shrieking out and the party was enveloped in a howling blizzard. Naseekayoosie's mother-in-law froze to death and his faithless wife came to him, crying, "Oh, Naseekayoosie, take pity on me! Save my life and I will be your slave even if you marry another woman." But no sound came from her husband's lips and she froze at his feet.

Only the old father-in-law was left of the family that had not heeded the leader's warning and was freezing. But the leader took pity on him and gave him warm fur clothing. Then, taking the old man on his own sled, the leader gave the signal and the journey continued.

At last the travelers reached a small village far from their old hunting grounds and the leader bade them build igloos, for this was to be their new home. Game was plentiful here and everybody now saw the great wisdom of their chief. They called him a great man and thereafter held him in their highest esteem. Everybody took a new interest in life and it was not long before all were again prosperous.

Several years passed and Naseekayoosie was beginning to forget his tragical first marriage. He had not intended to re-marry but one young woman of the village to which they had come attracted him and likewise did he attract her. They became lovers and not

long afterward were married with great ceremony. The villagers were glad that their leader was married and pleased with the wife he selected.

About a year later a baby girl was born to the young couple. Many presents were given to the baby and the village spent a week feasting, for Naseekayoosie was a rich man.

Then came the time when the child should be named. The young mother went to her husband and said, "Naseekayoosie, what was your mother's name? It is my wish that our daughter bear the same, that it be not forgotten."

"They called my mother Miginosie," said the husband.

"That is strange," returned his wife. "So was my mother, who died when I was a baby, called Miginosie."

Naseekayoosie thought of his little sister, who many years before had been carried away by strangers and never heard of since.

"What, then, was your father's name?" he asked anxiously.

"My father," answered the wife, "was the great Kioutayluk."

The words stunned Naseekayoosie to speechlessness. At last he cried out bitterly, "Oh, my wife, I have offended the earth and we shall be cursed. I, also, am the child of Kioutayluk!"

The unhappy couple knew not what to do! Innocently enough they had broken a sacred law of their race that permitted not even cousins to marry. Had it not been for the baby their disgrace would not have been so keen, at least it could have been more easily righted. Only one thing was left for them to do. They could carry their tragical discovery to the village council and abide by its decision.

The council met. Old men they were, of many years' experience, yet never had they had so hard a problem to solve. Many hours they thought, and pondered over, and discussed the case. At length they decided that since neither brother nor sister knew the identity of the other they had committed no intentional crime by marrying, so the tribe would not punish them. Still only a part of the problem had been solved. Then one day the council announced that it had reached a solution that would be satisfactory to man and earth. The people assembled in the kazhgie to hear it. When all was quiet an old gray-haired man arose and said, "There is but one way to do justice to these unhappy people and yet hold sacred the laws of our ancestors. Since this child is born of the children of Kioutayluk, it is of his blood, therefore, his daughter. It is only the sister and not the daughter of these people. As brother and sisters they may live together in honor."

Everybody was satisfied with this judgment. Surely, since this child had naught but the blood of Kioutayluk and Miginosie, it was their child, therefore a sister of their other children. Naseekayoosie was pleased with the council's wisdom for as a brother he could still share his home with his loved ones, no longer wife and child but sisters.

And so they lived until death took them to their parents. And as long as she lived, Miginosie never learned the secret of her birth.

HOW MR. RAVEN OUTWITTED THE FOX

For many years Mr. Raven and Mr. Red Fox had been very bitter enemies. The cause of their enmity was jealousy. Mr. Raven was the wisest of all the birds while Mr. Red Fox was known to be the most cunning of all the animals. Time and again each one had planned and schemed to bring about the other's downfall, always without success. But regardless of their hatred for each other, Mr. Raven and Mr. Fox always appeared to be on the best of terms.

One day Mr. Raven thought of a new scheme to rid himself of his rival and at the same time prove his superior wisdom to his friends. Going to Mr. Fox's igloo, he said, "Good morning, Mr. Fox. Let us go to the hill and play games."

Mr. Fox replied, "Very well, my friend. I will play slide-down-the-hill with you."

So they climbed a steep hill nearby and made ready to slide down the other side. Now this particular hill was so high that one could not see the deep pond at the bottom of it. But Mr. Raven knew it was there. And Mr. Fox did, too, but neither mentioned it.

"You go first," said the crafty Mr. Fox when all was ready. "I want to see how well you can slide."

"Very well," said the raven, and away he went. He slid so fast that he couldn't stop himself! But just as he was about to plunge into the pond at the bottom of the hill he spread his wings and glided across to the opposite side in safety. Then he called to the fox, "All right, Mr. Fox! Let's see how well you can slide!"

"No, I am afraid I might fall into the water," called the fox.

"Oh, no, you can't fall into the water," returned the raven. "Surely, you can jump as well as I can."

Mr. Fox was not to be outdone by a mere raven, however wise. If Mr. Raven had jumped the pond, he could too, so down he went. Down, down he slid so fast he couldn't stop himself. At the edge of the pond he made a mighty leap and landed right in the center of

the pool.

Mr. Raven's plan had worked out! He threw back his head and laughed wildly. "Help! help!" shouted the fox. "I am sinking!" But Mr. Raven only laughed and laughed as if he would die laughing and didn't stop until long after the fox had drowned.

WHAT DOES IT MEAN?

IGLOO is an Eskimo word for house or home. In Alaska most igloos are rectangular in shape and are dug about three feet into the ground. A floor of driftwood is laid, and side walls of driftwood erected vertically. The sloping roofs are also made of driftwood. There is sometimes an opening or window, which may be covered with seal or whale intestine, which admits light but is not transparent. To keep cold air out of the igloo, chunks of sod are cut out of the tundra and piled around the walls and on the roof. In winter, a hallway of similar materials is extended, away from the direction of the wind, from the door to an entry some distance from the building. Nowadays many Eskimos heat their homes with make-shift stoves burning wood or coal, and the stoves have an ordinary chimney. Each home also has a ventilator with a slide attachment to regulate the amount of air.

The dome-shaped igloo of snow blocks which is so often attributed to the Eskimo is made by only one group, which lives along the arctic shore of Canada near the mouth of the Mackenzie River.

OOGROOK is a large bearded seal. It often weighs 200 to 300 pounds.

PARKA is a fur garment built along the lines of the old fashioned night-shirt. It is pulled over the head, and reaches to the knees. A hood is attached which can be pulled over the head in cold weather, leaving only the eyes, nose and mouth exposed.

OOMIAK is a large boat, rowed by several people and carrying as many as twenty. It is made of walrus or oogrook skin, and its flexible sides make it easy to land against a rock or other hard surface, which would shatter an ordinary wooden boat.

CARIBOU is a wild animal related to the reindeer, which is native to Alaska and northern Canada.

CACHE is a food storage platform set high enough to be above the jumping range of wolves, bears or sled-dogs. There is one built alongside each igloo.

KAYAK is a small boat, usually used by one person. The boat is made of a driftwood frame covered with seal skin. The top skin is lashed tightly to a hoop which forms the frame of the cockpit, where the paddler sits. The boat is made practically watertight by lashing the paddler's gut rain parka to the outside of the cockpit frame. If the boat turns over, little water can get into the boat and the paddler can bring the boat upright, and go safely on his way. A second or third person can be in the boat fore or aft of the paddler, and completely covered.

KAZHGIE is a men's club, where all the men of the village assemble to discuss affairs. It is also the home of the bachelors of the village. In the old days the young were taught the customs of the village by listening to the stories of the old men at the Kazhgie.

MUKLUK is a boot of leather. The sole is often made of oogrook hide, and the leg part of seal or reindeer hide.

AU KOO TOOK is the Point Barrow term for so-called "Eskimo ice cream." The Shishmaref term is ka ma muk. This is a mixture of animal fat (melted reindeer fat, seal oil or other) to which is added dried blueberries or salmon berries and bits of dried meat and snow. The whole mixture is whipped to a cream-like consistency and is considered a great delicacy. There are many variations of the recipe.

More books on Eskimo life and tradition are available from
Alaska Northwest Books™, including:

The Roots of Ticasuk: An Eskimo Woman's Family Story, *by Ticasuk (Emily Ivanoff Brown).* This true, compelling account of generations of an Alaskan Native family tells of Eskimo traditions and the struggle to retain a proud culture. With map and photographs.
ISBN 0-88240-117-3, 107 pages/paperback, $9.95 ($12.95 Canadian)

I Am Eskimo: Aknik My Name, *by Paul Green, illustrated by George Aden Ahgupuk.* An Eskimo born at the turn of the century chronicles the old ways—from the proper use of *oogruk* (bearded seal) to "How Mama Eskimo make ice cream." With 75 drawings.
ISBN 0-88240-001-0, 86 pages/paperback, $12.95 ($15.95 Canadian)

Once Upon an Eskimo Time, *by Edna Wilder, illustrated by Dorothy Mayhew.* A remarkable 109-year-old Eskimo woman named Nedercook describes a year in the life of her Rocky Point village before the white man came. With 18 drawings.
ISBN 0-88240-274-9, 185 pages/paperback, $9.95 ($12.65 Canadian)

Ask for these books at your favorite bookstore, or contact us for a complete catalog.

Alaska Northwest Books™

A division of GTE Discovery Publications, Inc.
P.O. Box 3007
Bothell, WA 98041-3007
Toll free: 1-800-331-3510